Composition:

Confessions of an Altar Boy

by

Wayne J. Martin

2nd Edition

Publication, Press and Copyrights 2011, 2017
1sr Edition: October 21, 2011 &
2nd Edition: October 3, 2017

Confessions of an Altar Boy

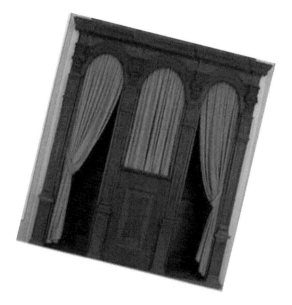

A slightly 'altared' confession

by

Wayne J. Martin

Excerpts

You would never see me without a baseball glove attached to my left hand or slung over my handlebars. Later in life I would replace the glove with a bottle of Corona.

In Catholic school you snickered a lot, laughter was not allowed. ... If a Catholic laughs he gets a slap in the back of the head. If a Jew laughs he slaps the back of his own head before his mother does. This is why you will see Catholics and Jews automatically grab the back of their heads when they laugh.

Maguire, McBurke and Morgan are still together today and still steeped in uncontrollable laughter. The only change is that the slap-baton has now been passed from the nuns to our wives.

Disclaimer

This book is based, in part, upon actual events, persons, and other entities. The characters, incidents and entities portrayed and the names used herein are fictitious. Any similarity of those fictitious characters, incidents, organizations or other entities to the name attributes or actual background of any actual person, living or dead, or to any existing entity, is entirely coincidental and unintentional.

Dedication

Without real-life experiences, any book would be empty.

For my classmates who were tortured, and scourged, and who bled and laughed with me, you have my deepest appreciation.

We offer our heartfelt apologies to those poor nuns who we tortured right back.

For the altar boys of Saint Mary's who were reverent when they needed to be, but found that one of God's greatest gifts is our ability to laugh.

To my best friends Tommy and Dennis, who made this entire journey with me, thanks for being smart and making that important. Thanks for your sense of humor and using it at the most inappropriate times.

Thank you to all of my friends from Islip High School for welcoming me and showing me that life can be a lot of fun after Purgatory.

To my older brother and sister for leading the way and to my younger brother for having the good sense to follow a different path; I love you guys very much.

To my best friend and wife Stephanie who had to reread every stinking version of every rewritten word of not only this book but my life. I love you. I love your way and everything about you.

Foreword

This is a collection of actual moments in my life that in some circles would be called *sins*. You may find this offensive and choose to quote Dorothy Parker, who once said of a book, "This is not a novel to be tossed aside lightly; it should be thrown with great force."

For the rest, I hope to open your eyes, your heart and exercise your right to laugh and snicker uncontrollably for that is my only goal.

This is a peek inside the odd mysteries of a parochial school. A *True Confession* tells all, hides nothing and is sincere. I do not wish to hide the fact that we cursed. From time to time I will introduce *bad words* as we called them. We did not curse in front of grown-ups and we never used what we called the 'f' word, really! Okay well almost never.

There is no plot. The only plot was to graduate and get out. If there is a message it is simply that parents can mold and guide their children, but it is their friends that shape who they become. I'll prove it to you. Who knows the real you, your parents or your friends? Parents would do better to manage their kid's friendships more closely and, by all means, feel free to smack them on the ass when it calls for it.

There will be a lot of references to fighting, being beaten up and the like. This is how boys grew up in the '50s and '60s. Our fathers thought it would toughen us up and make us men while mom took care of the more spiritual side of our life.

We were corporally punished by our teachers, our parents and more often by each other. We did not have virtual fighting or laws to over-protect us in those days. Real life doesn't offer such protection and I know, because of that, we were better prepared for what lies ahead.

I have provided a thorough **table of contents** for you for two good reasons:

✓ Since this book will be in the bathroom where it belongs,

✓ It will help you find your place when you return.

Table of Contents

Table of Contents

Table of Contents

Table of Contents

Table of Contents

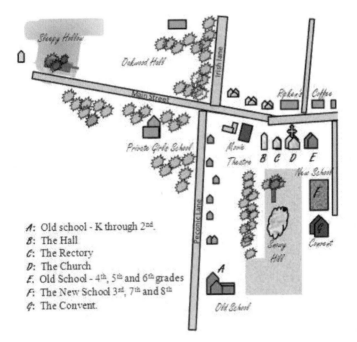

A: Old school - K through 2nd.

B: The Hall

C: The Rectory

D: The Church

E. Old School - 4th, 5th and 6th grades

F: The New School 3rd, 7th and 8th

G: The Convent.

Chapter, I mean,
Lesson 1: In the Beginning

My hands hang over my keyboard not daring to move. Something, something strange is near me and a cold shiver runs across my shoulders. My eyes move slowly to the right and then to the left, as if I am about to tell an ethnic joke. I am a bit nervous. You see I am about to tell all, to reveal a secret so closely held for so long a time, that there most certainly will be consequences.

The same mental scars and muscle memory cause another involuntary flinch. Surely the ghost of some nun is behind me loading up her right side with a yardstick. My wrists are pulling towards me in self-defense, and my fingers are curling up under my palms like frightened children. "Breathe!" I shout partly for myself and some to scare the ghost.

I unfold and slowly return my hands. I cautiously restart typing, peeking now and again over my shoulder. How can I be forgiven unless I confess this story, the whole story?

Naughty Boys

We were growing into our bodies. Our minds were taken over by our thoughts, a disturbing balance of prayer and sin. Our gazes drifted from the faces of the girls we once thought so cute, to their new curves that drew much closer inspection.

They started to sway as they walked and they were becoming beautiful to gaze upon. As they became more alluring, they were equally elusive. They were shaping themselves in a way that demanded attention, yet we found it harder to approach them. Our jokes were born not from experience but from that of abstinence. We substituted sexual humor and innuendo among ourselves to hide our tongue-tied frustration. We would huddle our laughter with a joker for a quarterback.

The nuns knew nothing of what made us laugh, but if we laughed, then it *must* be a sin. They were losing their grip on us. We were graduating after so many years. It was hard to believe that there really was an afterlife, a life after parochial purgatory, after the *Land of No*.

This is a doorway to take you to that place…a special place, back in time. It is like no other and has never been seen in public.

The Gathering

The open-minded diversity of a public school education is a risk to any church. It is here that a person may see or hear of another faith or seek a different truth.

Confessions of an Altar Boy

The last thing the Catholic Church wanted was for us to start with such a *heathen* public education. The church would say 'public school' with a look of disdain and then shake a bowed head. And so, they created their own version of kindergarten and the school years that followed. I remember my mother drove me to school that very first day. I was only four years and five months old.

It was a drab September day to fit the occasion, but my mother's dress was like a warm summer's garden. My mom always dressed up when she went out, all the women did in the fifties. She smelled like the flowers on her dress and her lipstick always found my cheek. To ensure my embarrassment, she would spit on a handkerchief and scrape the lipstick and the skin off my face.

Her face was round and she had dark wavy chestnut hair with blue eyes that constantly smiled at me. She was tall enough already, but her shoes made her taller. She was four months pregnant she would say, as she rubbed a tummy that barely cleared the steering wheel. I figured that meant she was eating too much. As we drove, we talked about a new brother or sister, which was very confusing. I had no frame of reference to put this new baby and the physical evidence together.

I was pretty well dressed up myself with a green plaid vest and a white shirt. I wore an uncomfortably tight black bow tie in contrast to my nearly white hair, but more about that later, we're here. Mom down-shifted our black Hudson and pulled slowly left off Peconic Lane. I could hear the tires spitting stones as we pulled across the dirt parking lot. A big house appeared out of nowhere. It was an old building even in 1954. I heard that some rich people donated it to the church because it was haunted. In reality, the Catholics bought it from the Episcopalians, but people take the versions they like best and make up their own history.

The big house was painted with what appeared to be ice cream, like if you mixed chocolate and vanilla together. It was tan. It was not smooth. It was made of stucco like my house, only bigger, much bigger. My mom said it was a Tudor-style. So I immediately looked at the doors and said, "Oh yeah!"

My mom smiled, "I meant the style, not the…oh never mind."

It had brown wooden trim like long chocolate bars as far as my eyes could see. I must have been starving that morning.

"Here we are!" Mom said more excited than would fit the occasion as she opened the car door. "Isn't this place beautiful?"

I did not answer right away. I felt like I was being dropped off at a baby sitter to be named later. A fairly accurate concern, so I figured to test the waters.

"How long do we have to stay here?"

"You'll be here all day like Richie and Julie," Mom said as she confirmed all of my suspicions. "Besides you'll make lots of new friends here, and you'll love it."

I squeezed out the barely audible but obligatory, "Yeah, sure."

The outer walls were covered with dark green ivy from the ground all the way to the eaves of the third floor. Someday I would think such things are classy and beautiful. At the age of four, it looked like something really neat to climb.

"Get off there! You'll get dirty!" as she pulled me down and brushed me off. "Can't you stay clean for two seconds!?" followed by a quick and deserved smack on the ass.

"Oh, Mom?" I complained.

I was glad that no one saw that. Okay. I figured, maybe I'll get to climb it later. But if the nuns were not enough to keep me off those vines, the yellow jackets were a much better watchdog. I hated bees and wasps. I learned that at school. Later that year, I would find that not all green leaves are alike and the sticky discomfort of calamine lotion. After that, the vines and I parted ways for good. These were important subjects not found in any classroom or graded on any report card, it was far more important than that. True learning is about life. It is a *gathering* of experiences. It is being able to separate fact from all else and to laugh at stupidity. Mostly it was about getting away with it.

Learning Parochial Style

I have no doubt that Robert Frost gets pissed and does a coffin-spin every time I refer to his, 'Road Not Taken.' I am sure his intention did not include the likes of me quoting him. Still, I think it is the best poem ever written and describes my existence perfectly.

> I shall be telling this with a sigh
> Somewhere ages and ages hence:
> Two roads diverged in a wood, and I—
>
> I took the one less traveled by,
> And that has made all the difference.

This has become important to me and has helped me survive because sometimes the path leads to trouble and you need to blame someone, it might as well be Frost. There were also some smart choices in life that we made and thank God we did. After 9 years of masochistic pleasure, we decided to continue our education at a public school. This was a time much better told than lived.

Holy Days of Obligation

I envied my Jewish and Protestant friends. When there was a holiday, they would get the entire day off from school with no further obligations whatsoever. As parochial school students, we had no outlet. If you were off from school for some holiday, it was probably a *holy day*. After all, the word holiday stems from holy day. We had to go to church while those freakin' heathens frolicked and played, usually in front of my house.

"Hey, Wade, where ya' going? We're going to start a baseball game!"

"I've got to go to church," I was obliged to answer as part of the pathetic teasing ritual.

"It's not Sunday!" Lenny would turn to Charlie. "It's not Sunday, is it?"

"It's a holy day," I was thinking how they were milking this one.

"What time will you be back?"

"About ten."

"Oh, we'll probably be done by then." Lenny loved to rub it in.

I rolled the window up as we left. The adults did not seem to mind church at all. Of course, they were too old to play baseball so what else did they have to do. It was not bad enough that half the weekend was spent in church. Once in a while, to piss me off, a holy day would come on a Saturday. This cancels out the weekend entirely. I don't care what religion or size you were, you would do well to stay away from me on one of those days.

"Hey, *Wade*, where ya' goin'?" someone would yell outside of rock throwing distance.

"Come over here. I can't hear you," as I picked up a choice stone.

Then they would say something consoling like, 'Hurry back' while keeping their distance and waving a sadistic smile. After we were out of earshot, one of them would fire off a 'poor bastard' followed by a few sympathy nods.

Some kids were faster than others. The big ones could get away with teasing the crap out of me. Either way, I would get them on the baseball field. I'll be on third, and Lenny will cover first. I'll throw him a ball that comes up about three feet short. He'll turn his head and he'll take one off the ear. It seemed I daydreamed too often, especially about revenge and humor. Church was a quiet place to plan things out like, while firing off a few prayers.

Road Less Traveled

Even while at school we had all sorts of reasons to attend church: the first Friday of every month or the Bishop was coming. Who knew? The nuns loved to parade us over to the church.

"We are going over to the church today as the choir has learned a new song."

"Good freakin' grief."

"What did I just hear!?"

"Good. Really neat, sister!"

It seemed there were too many excuses to get us out of class for one of their habit-huddles. It was far better than having to teach us. We knew their angle. We would kneel while the nuns whispered in socialized prayer. In their protective habits, you could still see them turning to

8

whisper to each other. Right in the middle of service!!! What I would not have given to see Mother Superior come up and smack one of them in the back of the head! See how they liked it.

"Pay attention!" Mother Superior would yell.

Then she would reach into sister's head piece, grab her by the ear and march her down the aisle. Ah, I had such beautiful daydreams. I noticed that we spent more and more time in church and less in school. When we were in school, we learned important things.

"Columbus discovered America in 1492. He was a Catholic," the nun read from our perfectly edited history book.

Then we would have a test to see if we remembered that he was a Catholic.

We had the same teacher, usually a nun, all day long. She taught different subjects. In reality, she taught religion under the name of different subjects. We had another subject actually called Religion and we'd have a test on that too.

"Are we having a test today, Sister?"

"Every day is a test young man."

"Yes, Sister."

If that nun were Jewish, she would have answered my question with a question. "Why is today different from any other day"?

All of this selective education ensured that we were socially illiterate in case we ever went on to public school or had a conversation with a Jew or a Protestant. Some of our friends opted to continue with a Catholic high school education thereby creating a difficulty in seeing outside of the poor box. They would walk through the rest of their lives with swollen wrists and knuckles known as *Corporal Tunnel Syndrome.*

Somewhere down this *road less traveled*[1] New York State intervened and made the parochial schools teach science and music. Saint Mary's felt that it was important to get a music teacher from the outside. They did not feel the same urgency for science. There is nothing like being taught science by a nun who was born before Copernicus and believed Darwin a heretic. Let us not forget that the earth was created in seven days about 5,000 years ago. They looked intelligent from a distance, but then their words reached our ears. At least that proved that light is faster than sound.

When we finally evolved into a public high school, we were immediately put into a remedial science class to undo the damage.

Some people lose their way depriving some small town of their idiot.

-   *unknown*

---

[1] Excerpt from "Road Not Taken," a poem by Robert Frost.

The Snicker

One of God's greatest gifts is laughter, and Satan's gift is to instill in us, a sense of bad timing.

A more up to date example of the snicker can be witnessed, but barely heard in the movie Pretty Woman[2]. Richard Geer is a great snickerer. He would have made a good Catholic. Maybe he had some formal training. Geer brings this snicker to every one of his films. He can't help it. It is like a tick, a terrible habit (*habit... snicker*). See what I mean? Snickering was a valuable weapon if you were going to survive the dungeon built by the stone hands of the School Sisters of Our Lady.

A snicker is a nasal sound mostly, like exhaling through one's nose. It comes when trying to hide a laugh, but the air leaks out. Hey, it has to go somewhere. It is often acceptable to let some of the air escape out of the sides of your mouth. A snicker must be done properly: too restricted and you could blow an ear drum, too heavy and unwanted bodily fluids and other projectiles may be hurled with shirt-bound accuracy. It is important to release the tension of the moment properly without messing someone's clothes. If you have a cold or a stuffy nose you best release the snicker entirely out the sides of your mouth ...please.

---

[2] Pretty Woman is a 1990 romantic comedy film. Written by J.F. Lawton and directed by Garry Marshall, the film stars Richard Gere, Julia Roberts and Hector Elizondo.

In Catholic school you snickered a lot, laughter was not allowed. I'll remind you of that from time to time because many of you are not "of the faith" and you may forget. If a Catholic laughs, he or she gets a slap in the back of the head. If a Jew laughs, he slaps the back of his own head before his mother does. This is why you will often see Catholics and Jews automatically grab the back of their heads when they laugh.

The Sneeze

"So's your old man?"

"Hey screw you and the freakin' horse you rode in on!"

After a weekend of fast and loose with your buddies, you had to downshift your language come Monday morning. We were good at it. But there are times when no other words could describe the moment. Substitutions like heck for hell, darn for damn and freakin' for …well, you get it. You could get by at home with those, but even these lame substitutions were not allowed in school. The ultimate was to sneak a real one out and get away with it. Ah, we lived for those moments. And as our teacher started our history lesson, we all leaned forward and the following exchange would take place.

"Alexander Fleming, who was a devout Catholic, discovered Penicillin due to divine intervention."

"Horseshit," I managed to sneeze. "Excuse me, sister."

"God Bless you."

"Thank you, sister."

And she could not understand the laughter that ensued. But the *horseshit, bullshit, anything-shit* was used to express our need to critique as protected by the first amendment. I thought it ironic that we called it History. I don't care if it was called 'Her Story.' It was certainly somebody's story. One thing is for sure, it was indeed worth a good sneeze-critique.

Washington said. "I cannot tell a lie."

Pass me a freakin' hanky. I feel another one coming on.

Lesson 2: The Boys of St. Mary's

Isn't there something about laughter at the wrong time? The most trivial prank becomes a masterpiece, if the solemn timing is wrong. Here I have gathered the masters of their trade, artisans, each one of them. They honed their skills like cannibal-chefs working the kettle and timing their stirs with perfection.

Nicknames stuck and if you did not pick one worthwhile one would be found for you. Kids that were quick with their wit and fists walked freely; the others stepped lightly in fear of what the day might bring. We referred to everyone by their last names unless you were speaking to them directly, then you would use their nickname. This practice was very wisely reversed when speaking to a nun.

Here are some notables, the names that they earned and why.

Backer

"My name is Backer. James Backer. You can call me Jimmy, or Backer. Don't call me James. If you call me *James*, I'll kick your ass. Understood?"

He was lean and mean to any kid who stopped his stride. He looked like a younger, slimmer version of today's Matt Dillon[3]. He had brown hair and slits for eyes. They were so closed they would not reveal any color and when he laughed, they shut completely. He laughed at pain, not his, other people's.

He once stabbed Mike in the palm fooling around one day in class. I am making this sound worse than it was. The rest of us did not carry knives. I am also making Jimmy sound worse than he was because that's how Jimmy would have wanted it. By the way, that was the one and only stabbing incident we ever had. Mike did not tell. It was a minor puncture and he made up a story so the nurse would fix it. Backer thought I was funny and he liked having my arm on his team for the snowball fights. This was my 'in.' His only humorous thought was how we were going to torture somebody. He didn't laugh at jokes. You need not embarrass yourself by trying, he only laughed at the misfortunes of others.

He was an altar boy too so you can see how picky they were. If there were a football team, he would have been our captain. We would have had no choice. With all of

---

[3] Matt Dillon. Nee Matthew, Actor, February 18, 1964. Originally teen actor, Matt usually played troubled youth rolls.

that overhead, there was still something decent and likable about him, as you will see.

Robbins

"My name is Steven *why-don't-you-just-beat-me-up-right-now* Robbins." This is one of those rules we had talked about. If you did not properly shorten your name or get a nickname you were going to get the ever-loving crap knocked out of you. A simple 'Steve' would have saved him from a world of pain. The formal, 'Steven', was unacceptable.

Steven had light brown hair, lips far too red for a guy, glasses and two huge ears to rest them upon. These were all framed within an oval head. I think his family sued Mr. Potato Head for copyright infringement. He was easily entertained. You could get him into a laughter-frenzy at the drop of someone else's hat. He would go into a red-faced, collar-burning seizure of laughter that he could not possibly stop. Well, except maybe by a scowl from Backer.

"Hey! What are YOU laughing at?" then he'd shut down faster than congress on recess.

Steven would often find his name written down for detention on the blackboard. We were supposed to write our own names down, but it was a lot more fun to write his instead. At the end of the day, Sister Zelda would shake her head and try to remember what poor Steven had done. Coming up empty was her normal state so she would keep him after with the rest of us. I'd have to say he was a good sport about it. Maybe he liked staying and thought we put his name down so he could join us. Just to make things worse, his mom was a permanent substitute teacher. At least my mom had stopped doing that after third grade. I remember that Steven's father had passed away in those years. I had not lost anyone close to me in those days, and it touched home with all of us. Backer said, "Hands off (Steven) from now on."

We all agreed. You see, I told you there was something about Jimmy. I like to call this, the softer side of the Backer (not out loud of course).

We called Robbins, Steve from then on whether he liked it or not. We still wrote his name down on the board though. It was our way of saying, "Welcome."

Due to our fine boot camp, I am figuring that he became either an auditor or a retired mass murderer by now. At least I hope he's retired.

Fagan

Joseph Fagan. "Joseph?" Here we go again. As a point of reference, we had a friend in our neighborhood named Joey Hagan. See how close two names could be? They were nothing alike, however. Hagan was smaller. If you called him Joseph you'd be nursing a bloody nose. He was cool. So why 'Joseph' Fagan? One can only shake their head. I mean, hang up another 'Beat Me Up' sign, already.

Joseph was about my size. He probably wore the same size shirt as me. His chest was good, but his arms stuck out like two undeveloped sticks. He wore his pants way too high. He was like Robbins but more on the serious side. His hair was darker and he wore no glasses. To compound the issue, Joseph wore a hat with ear-muffs. I am sorry, this is begging for it. And, man oh man did he get it. We would chase him so far down Peconic Lane a taxi could not get him back from recess on time. The upside was that he would get to stay after school with 'the boys.' Now he was cool.

Fagan was good at anything he tried; he just wasn't into sports at that time. I started calling him Joey whether he liked it or not. He needed a little push in the right direction. I would stop over his house to have a catch which was okay since he was Joey now.

"I'm going to Joey's house, Mom!"

"You mean Joseph Fagan?"

"No Mom, JOEY Fagan. Please call him Joey. It's important."

I could see my mom telling the neighborhood that I went over to Joseph's house. I'd have a beating and a pile-on waiting for me when I got home. Fagan moved into the non-pick zone after that. He put away the ear muffs, got himself a glove, caught a seasonal cold, got the 'I told you so' from his mom and was now like the rest of us. He filled out a bit and became a regular guy, still quiet but regular. I am not sure where Joey is now. I am sure that he is successful and can tackle anything you throw at

19

him. We prepared him for that. Surely Hallmark has a Thank You card he should send us.

Petty

Petty, Bobby. Just plain Petty would do. He was a strange magician. He did not make things disappear. He was a comedian that did not tell jokes. He was a clown, but he wore no paint, and he would never touch a balloon unless he had a pin. But what he did have was antics. He had them down to a science. He was slim built and his head was narrow. He had straight blonde hair and brown eyes shielded by wire-rimmed glasses. His height was at least average and he looked destined to become a rock star. It was not easy to make him laugh so stirring him into uncontrollable convulsions was not possible, unless you fell or were getting beaten up by a nun. His total control took a lot of fun out of retaliation because he could certainly stir the pot toward your detention. This was especially true in church or when you were trying to read aloud. The more solemn the moment, the more powerful his magic became.

Maguire

Dylan Maguire was first alphabetically in what we called our 3M Company at St. Mary's. He is the oldest by a few months. So it would seem he would be first at many things along the way.

A contradiction in the scheme of things was the name, *Dylan*. This is not really a nickname. This was an exception to the nickname rule. You could get away with such things, especially, when your fist was quick and ready. If that were not enough, he came from Brooklyn, which to us islanders was part of 'the City.' You did not mess with guys from 'the City.' We were both slim and wiry, but he was always taller with a touch of freckles, which gave away his Irish beneath a dark-haired disguise. His blue eyes told everything from a readiness to fight, to love, to laugh or cry the tears of snickering or unbridled laughter.

Dylan had a great technique, but he did not own the snicker. We all had that down pat (*ooh, innuendo opportunity here*). What he did own was the whisper. He was the undisputed 'King of the Whisper.' He was like the Green Arrow[4], but he shot off whisper-darts, instead. He would pull back the volume with a sharpened wit to ensure his target and only his target.

He would nock his arrow as you were staring into the face of a nun. His dart was now loaded. With a quick wit and a smooth release, a perfect whisper was sent in your direction, you were toast. He would drive your snicker into uncontrollable convulsions right in the puss of a nun. Now bound for detention, you could join him at the end

---

[4] Green Arrow is a fictional super-hero, published by DC Comics in 1941 by Mort Weisinger and George Papp. He is an archer, who invents trick arrows with various special functions.

of the day. It is still impossible, to this day, for Dylan and I to sit together without reminiscing ourselves into side splitting seizures. We will continue to join each other in laughter for the rest of our lives and beyond, in that great detention in the sky. Oh okay, smart-ass, it may not be in the sky, but wherever it is, we'll be there and we will save you a freakin' seat!

McBurke

Todd McBurke was the youngest member of the 3Ms, not first alphabetically but definitely in size and arguably the smartest. Not an ounce of fat about him, broad and lean. He outsized most the class and even Jimmy, "don't call me James" Backer, who cast an eye and a reassuring nod to Todd when he walked by. Like Dylan, he threw right and batted left. A more current resemblance would yield a view of Phil Mickelson[5] at age twelve.

His wavy blonde hair, thick bottom lip and blue eyes were frames to accent the absolute Master of the Smirk. He had a great smile that he could ratchet down into that perfect grin. He would cock his head at a purposely odd angle to set you off balance and look down the aisle at you. Not a word need be spoken, but the intent was there. He looked like he was going to lose it at any moment …any moment now… and then, it was not him,

---

[5] Philip Alfred Mickelson (born June 16, 1970) is an American professional golfer. He is nicknamed "Lefty" for his left-handed swing, even though he is otherwise right-handed

but you, who lost it. So was it written and so was his plan. If coupled in harmony with a Dylan whisper dart, not even Petty, himself, could stay in control.

Todd was only betrayed by his Irish complexion, as it would turn him beet-red at the drop of a snicker. Maybe we could have labeled him the Red Lantern, as the color in his face crept over him like a Maraschino cherry. While others went into convulsions, Todd was a thermometer ready to explode. His red face sent up a flare to the nuns that a slap was in order. I cannot recall Todd ever executing any trouble. His enormous vocabulary would weave a new antic and even cast the characters. Then he would sit back like a director. He had a way of keeping its momentum and it seemed to erupt around him like a tsunami. It would have been nice if he yelled 'cut' once in a while. All of his intellect and cleverness never escaped the nuns and his name was on the detention board right next to his snickering buddies.

I could not get enough of this, so we went on through high school and we even roomed together in college . . . for a while anyway. I could not study with him smirking all the time, so I flunked out after the first year.

Morgan

Wade Morgan. What can I say about myself? I wasn't born first. I was born in the middle. I fell between Todd and Dylan in age in our 3M Company. It was someone's job to be shortest, so I filled that spot nicely.

My friend Jack used to tell me, "Wade, avoid frustrations and disappointments, set low goals for yourself."

I was born with a warning-track power frame. I probably would have done well to take his kind advice at least once in a while. Tall guys never got called punk. I had to be ready to fight, and since I was always ready, I rarely had to. That and the fact that I had big friends did not hurt any. I was much more ready to laugh and cause laughter. What Todd did with his smirk and Dylan with his whispers, I did with my words. I had no volume control knob and apparently no on/off switch either.

I would think of funny things at the wrong time, blurt them out, and then the nuns would put me away in a corner. Surely strangers thought that I should be put away. Actually, people who know me wonder. "Who the hell let him out?" This started in kindergarten and it has never stopped.

You would never see me without a baseball glove attached to my left hand or slung over my handlebars. Later in life, I would replace the glove with a bottle of Corona. The nuns could not keep my attention. I was prone to gaze off into the distance. I would read a page from a book, but before I got halfway down the page, my mind was off somewhere else. Whenever the class read in silence, I was always the last to finish. I could barely remember what I read. I had a great ear for understanding and an acute sense of the questions and right answers. They would come from nowhere that I can explain. I was mathematical and it got me through with some good grades. There is no doubt they would label me ADD if I were in school today. What I could never figure out was why the school did not separate the three M's. It would have most definitely saved them an inordinate amount of pain.

Maguire, McBurke and Morgan are still together today and still steeped in uncontrollable laughter. The only change is that the slap-baton has now been passed from the nuns to our wives.

Post

William Post, 'Bill' or just 'Post' rarely got in trouble, but was always in the middle of it. He was taller, but then who wasn't? He had brown hair and freckles. He sparked trouble like a match. We would be out at recess without a plan and Post would inject, "How about we..." and whatever followed was surely going to get us in trouble. We would do it anyway. He could stir the pot with Petty and strut like Bailey, but walk away without so much as a scratch or his name on the back blackboard.

I had to figure him for the driver in a big jewelry heist one day. We call him Maui Bill today. Hmm, Maui, eh? Maybe he finally got away with the 'Big One.'

Bailey

Edward Bailey, Big Ed or more commonly known as, Bailey. No one called him Ed unless you and he were talking alone or we were trying to disrupt his reading aloud. Bailey had an average build but was very very tall. He towered over Todd and Dylan. I am not sure he could even see me from up there. At times, the clouds parted and I am pretty sure that he had light brown hair and some kind of eyes. I could do a lot of stories on Ed, but the most notable was his *Bailey Strut*. This was more than an event or an antic, it was an attitude.

To do the Bailey Strut, you had to cop this *attitude* in your step. Stand up tall! Your gaze must be maintained above the entire class. It was as if you do not care. You didn't even care about what others thought, they were, after all, beneath you. Bailey didn't even care whether or not he cared. Each step in the strut was pronounced, not long, not short, but slow enough, with an almost procession-like bounce that demanded attention. Your arms were an integral part of the strut. They needed to hang down locked at the elbows which were open yet only slightly away from your frame. It was critical that they remain still like in a river dance, but with your palms up as if the world was about to grace you with a reward.

Your fingers flickered slightly as if to say, "You can pay me now for giving you the exalted pleasure of letting you view my presence."

I think you should all practice the Bailey Strut at home in the mirror. Then try this at work or the next time you enter your in-law's house. You could report back to me on how you did. After all, this is an important piece of American History.

Kevin K

Kevin Kwztkowski. Make a note of it, I will not write that last name again. It is too painful. You would never refer to Kevin by his last name. The first time I saw it, I thought someone dropped some scrabble pieces. I lived on a street with the Smiths, the Jones and the Nelsons. He pronounced it once for me. I gave it the old, "Yeah sure," and just called him Kevin. If you can't spell it, then you certainly can't pronounce it.

Kevin was a bit taller than I. What a surprise there! He had straight dark hair and I believe his eyes were a dark brown. His head was definitely not built for a football helmet. It was wider at the top and narrowed to a nearly pointed chin. He was thin like most of us who were active. None of this means a rat's ass. What matters is that Kevin did things differently, unlike anyone else I ever knew. Like the guy speeding in and out of traffic, Kevin had a way of drawing attention to himself.

He obviously had no fear of getting hurt. I am not sure the thought of failure ever entered his mind. The pleasure of his company was only exceeded by his entertainment value which should have been labeled, Do Not Try This at Home. He was a legend at Sleepy Hollow, one of our favorite spots. I think there may be a plaque there in his name. Come to think of it, a custom helmet might not have been a bad idea. You will see what I mean later.

Education is always about the perfect scenario. Real life is always about the exception.
Stephanie Martin, December 28, 2009

Lesson 3: The Girls of St. Mary's

We spent so much time with them: the "Guhrls" as Sister Agnes called them. But nothing comes to mind quicker than our principal's famous "bathing speech" with her pompous New England drawl.

"The boys seem to be dressing nicer, but the guhrls, the guhrls, the dirty, dirty, dirty guhrls! They need to bathe. She shook her head in disgust. "I bathe every single day!" she said.

"No wonder she looks like a prune," Dylan sent one of his darts to my ear.

A locomotive hiss of an unchecked snicker has let go from within me. People stare at me. I gave them the 'I'll kill you look,' and they turned away.

She continues, "I want to see the guhrls bathing every day before they come to school."

"Me too," I said toward Dylan a little too loudly.

Damned volume control! Laughter erupts around us.

She is off in the distance and does not notice the wave as the jokes pass through the crowd. Her lecture continues for another ten torturous minutes. It is funny, but before this day I had always thought that she favored the girls over us. They never got into trouble or had to stay after school.

The girls wore white and light blue plaid skirts, white blouses with a navy blue vest, dark blue knee high socks and to add to their safely guarded look, a dark ribbon tie. They may not have looked good to Prune-face, but they sure looked great to us.

"A man may be a fool and not know it, but not if he is married."
---H.L. Mencken

The Giggle

In the beginning, they were nothing more to us than an audience for our daily antics. I would say that around 4th grade, however, all of that changed. One by one, they slipped into our lives. It seemed that they spent their time in groups of three or four but no more than five. They'd stand at the edge of the play yard like they were waiting for a bus. If you drew near them, they would huddle like a football team with two quarterbacks.

You could hear two of them talking about different subjects at the same time. I'd get a headache if I listened to that all day. They had secrets and spent much of their time leaning into each other's ears. They would stop when we walked by and when you were about eight and three-quarter feet away, they'd giggle.

"Hey, that was too early," I heard one snap when the other fired off a premature giggle.

"Sorry, I couldn't help it."

"Well, watch it!"

Early or not, it made a guy very insecure. I walked over to Todd Fix.

"Is there anything on the back of my pants?" I'd ask.

"Nope."

I had so much trust in Todd Fix that I got a second opinion from one of the younger kids.

"Nope."

Then I'd go check the mirror. Nothing. What the hell is with those girls anyway? As guys, we had no fair retort for the giggle and they knew it tortured us. Once in a while, we would go too far. We would make snide comments to each other and burst out into sidesplitting pandemonium. This would send a girl running back to the gaggle crying her eyes out.

This was a bit extreme and we would only resort to this after three or four unanswered giggles. It was worth it watching them spinning around checking out each other's clothes. Now that over forty years have gone by I can tell you what I have learned about 'the giggle.' Not a damn thing, nothing! I have no idea.

The Name of the Game

Once in a while, one girl would break away from her crowd and walk right up to us. Lana was not afraid of us in the slightest.

"Belinda likes you," she said to Dylan.

"That's nice," Dylan said, looking at us.

The element of surprise gave us no time to kid him about it. We were unprepared. Dylan looked at us and shrugged his shoulders. In the days that followed, we would catch Dylan and a red-faced Belinda leaving the clothes closet in the back of the classroom.

Each day Lana would come over like a newspaper boy with the latest "Read all about it" in the *Who Likes Who Gazette*. Her shoulder length dark hair was a nice contrast to the Irish freckles. She was a bit of a tom-boy which only made her that much more attractive. She wasn't as frilly as the other girls and you could have a catch with her if you had an extra glove.

"And who does Lana like?" I tried to fluster her as she was walking away.

And without missing a step or a beat, she turned and said, "Todd, of course."

"Which one, Fix or McBurke?" we asked.

"Guess," she tossed the comment back with a flick of her hair.

The spear had been thrust at our feet and there were no peace feathers upon it. It was as if someone shot off a starter's pistol. *"Let the games begin!"*

According to the Code

She seemed to pop up out of nowhere, but she would hold your gaze for quite some time. Her high cheeks framed her smile like rose parentheses, and her eyes glistened under shining chestnut hair. Her skin was pure silk and she was one hundred percent cute. She looked like a chipmunk but was quieter than a church mouse. And if you told her that, her quick feet would find your shins and they would be bloodier for the effort.

Her name was Christine and she became Dylan's girlfriend in fifth grade. She lived a mile in the opposite direction from school and Dylan would go to her house on Saturdays. After collecting enough dents in his shins, Dylan moved on and found another pretty heartthrob closer to home with slower feet.

According to our code, I asked Dylan before pursuing Christine. She wasn't much into notes and our conversations were limited. I'd see her briefly at recess, poke some fun at her, get my shins kicked and make plans for the next Saturday.

I went to her house and we played kickball, naturally, to sharpen her skills. Since neither of us drove, we met at parties. When we went roller-skating, our mom's would drop us off. I loved dancing with her and she smelled as pretty as she looked, but after a number of months of those exhausting conversations with no shin-guards we drifted apart. After about seven months of no contact

33

whatsoever, Lana, the town crier, came over to me with the latest off the presses.

"Christine says she doesn't want to be your girlfriend anymore," she hesitated and turned to Todd, "She said she'd like to go out with you now, Todd."

"No, thanks," he said so matter-of-factly, I nearly had a snicker-mishap.

I guess her plan was to date the entire 3M Company. It was not to be. Me? I can still run my hands up and down my shins and feel the dents of Christine.

Barbara Hatch

I'll treat this one as delicately as we would have in the day. We were all returning from what seemed to have been a very long summer vacation. Anticipation will do that. This was to be our 8th grade and final year at Saint Mary's which would make us the oldest and the masters of all we burned and pillaged.

I lived in Littleton as did a number of us, but the majority of kids lived in East Littleton. During the summer we had no contact with each other except for Little League or a sideways nod in church. It would seem that some would grow faster than others.

Barbara left the seventh grade as a twelve-year-old, but she walked into eighth grade at what must have been sixteen. It took a while to recognize her. She was taller. She had a brand spanking new uniform. She had to! Her vest protruded far away from her tummy, which now seemed incredibly thin under her chest and over those perfect hips. The other girls were developing too but not like this. She must have swallowed the magic beans.

Guys were rubber-necking over the aisles and spoke sideways to each other while their eyes never lost sight. We must have appeared like those paintings, no matter where she moved we were looking right at her. I think Barbara was embarrassed, but every single one of us made a point to welcome her back, and yes, with open arms. Every one of the guys I mean. Meanwhile, the rest of the girls circled around their saucers of milk. During recess, we could talk about nothing else.

"I always liked her," we each would say, but it was too late to try to stake any claim. She would be going out with older guys now. We had no chance.

It took a while to get used to. Time itself stood still when she walked by. The other girls would shortly follow suit as they seemed to grow every day and migrate Barbara slowly back into their competition, I mean, friendship.

Bless me, Father, for I have sinned....I have had bad thoughts a number of times this week...

Lesson 4: After School

Parties

Part rebellion and part new found freedom, it seemed like we were getting away with something. It was a party. It was a *No-Nuns-Allowed* party, not at school but at someone's house! They were almost always due to someone's birthday. The usual fan-fare of hot dogs, burgers, cake and Coca-Cola were served. My mother did not work, but she distributed Avon from the house, so I always had some perfume to bring to these parties. I didn't know if it was any good or not. Mom even had stuff for men.

"It's not perfume, it's cologne," she'd say.

"I'm not giving a guy perfume no matter what you call it."

I would ditch that and buy them a record or something. Looking back, I may have been the very first homophobe. I could almost hear the History Lesson, "Did you know that the first homophobe was a Catholic?"

The girls all wore something different, unlike their boring uniforms for school. They had party dresses and their ankles and calves were showing. They had blouses with no bow ties and open necks.

They had jewelry and perfume and, "Ho…ho…holy crap!! Is that makeup?"

And contrary to the ravings of Sister Mary "I-bathe-every-day" Agnes, the girls were clean and they smelled good too. All of a sudden I realized something about them that I had not noticed before; they were making me very nervous. Before the Beatles, we played and danced the Lindy. Later they invented dances to separate the girls from the boys and they were called the Twist and the Mashed Potato. These were easier than the Lindy, so they caught on fast. I liked the slow dances.

We slow danced and held the girls pretending we knew how. Dancing with a girl was as easy as asking, that is to say, not that easy at all. The more the girl meant to you the tougher it was, especially the asking part. Rejection is hard enough, but public rejection created scars.

The girls were always in groups as were the guys. You had to leave the security of your group and make your way across the floor. You would not be stupid enough to excuse yourself, you would casually slip away. Not a soul would notice you had moved, but slipping back into your group was impossible. You had to be willing to take the chance. If you had a girl there that you liked, you had better take that chance. A lot depended on the degree. The less you cared, the more confident you looked and, yes, the reverse was also true. I had not started dating Christine yet.

"Hey Wade, there she is! Are you going to ask her to dance?"

So much for a sly exit.

"Yeah, sure, maybe. I'm going to get a coke or two first."

There is nothing like a few stiff ones to give you confidence. I used the excuse to make my way across the floor. Before I got half way across someone else asked her. She said yes and now I am stuck. I am trapped in this limbo and not the limbo with a pole.

"Great."

I must have looked stoned drunk as I headed toward her side of the room then making a right toward the soda. There was no hiding. You either got the dance or walked the plank back through the laugh gauntlet. Everyone knew but no one, more than you.

"Looks like you blew it."

"Oh, I only wanted a coke. There'll be other songs."

"Sure you did. Hey, don't worry about it."

I wanted to throw myself in front of a bus. Now if I asked her, and she said no, I'd really look like a jerk. But I did, she didn't, and we danced and we danced for months.

"The man who can't dance thinks the band is no good."
---Polish Proverb

On Sleepy Hollow Pond

It was so late in spring you could smell summer. It was in the warmth of the sidewalk and the trees were nearly full out. Even if you had to stay after school, there was plenty of light left in the day. It cultivated idle time. And the nuns referred to "idle time" as our playground. After our Saturday altar boy meeting, we would enjoy the long bike ride home by stopping somewhere along the way.

One of our great entertainment spots was a place called Oakwood Hall, also known as Sleepy Hollow Lake. It had a pond with streams and was carefully and beautifully bulk-headed. This was a great place for games like tag, hide-and-seek, or our all-time classic favorite, *Watching Kevin Get Hurt*.

If there's a big hole filled with slimy green water, Kevin will always find it. He'd be running and then he'd suddenly disappear. A strange plunger-like sound would be followed by a loud scream as Kevin would proclaim his new find.

"Help, get me out! Somebody get me out!"

Lassie was not around so Todd or Dylan would have to find a branch and throw it to him. Sometimes, when we weren't looking for added entertainment, we'd actually hold the other end of that branch. I would just watch because, hey, someone had to write all of this down. If it wasn't a hole or being clothes-lined by some poor unsuspecting vine, you could watch Kevin *almost* make the jump across the stream. The obligatory mid-air exclamation of, "Oh shit!" was the only sound that preceded his shins bouncing off the wooden bulkhead.

He had to crawl out of the stream the long way. At least the cold water eased some of his pain as he limped his way to the shore line. His clothes were now totally soaked, but at least they were clean of the green slime of his previous encounter. He rolled his pants legs up. Two golf-ball like bumps emerged under his scraped skin. I still cringe when I think about it. This is something that you would do only once, well most of us.

"Good thing you're not going out with Christine!" I tried to console him.

"Oh, Wade!?" Dylan often complained about my poor timing.

"Thanks," was all Kevin would say as he nursed his brand new shin-testicles.

His entertainment value alone was enough to count him as one of our closest friends. If Kevin weren't with us, we'd go right by Sleepy Hollow without stopping. I mean, what would be the point?

Soccer

There weren't a lot of extracurricular sports at St. Mary's. We didn't have a regular baseball team every year. And so each year we would try a different sport, one year we gave soccer a chance.

The one thing they did right was that they got us a great coach. His name was Mr. Duffy. He was direct from

Ireland. I think that made him twice as Catholic as the rest of us. Anyway, he could teach us this new game. He was an average sized man, a bit on the thin side. He had a touch of gray around the edges to give him that mature, *don't I look like a real coach* look. And of course, there was that accent.

We had drills and exercises and it was tough. I mean we all wanted to see how far we could kick the ball. He wanted us to nudge it like a fairy and then pass it to someone else so they could fairy it down the field. We finally got it though. You fairy it down the field until another kid from the other team gets in front of you. You lure him in and when he gets close, you kick it as hard as you can right at him. This will make him think twice the next time the 'chicken' contest occurs and that is real Irish soccer, Duffy-Style. This was our interpretation anyway. We had assigned positions on the field. Mr. Duffy would explain where each of us was stationed and what we should do.

"Ya' understand it now boyz?"

We all nodded our heads in agreement. "Yes. Mr. Duffy."

"There ya' go then."

Once the game began, we'd forget all that and gang up on the ball.

Mr. Duffy would bounce up and down at the sidelines shaking his hands in the air as he shouted, "One a yuz now, boyz, one a yuz!"

We could not figure out what the hell he was saying. I mean, Okay, but which one of us? Naturally, I knew he was talking to me and telling the rest of the kids to let me have the ball.

Nobody scored a goal, but we won anyway because we had more kids left at the end of the game than they did. Mr. Duffy went back home to Ireland after only one year for some reason.

No big deal, we'd get a new sport next year.

You're never too old to learn something stupid.
-   Unknown

Track

The next year we tried track. It wasn't soccer and it certainly wasn't baseball. In fact, it did not even have a ball at all. You ran around this big circle to see who wins. How lame. Sometimes you only got to run around part of the circle after someone handed you a stick. Even more lame! What kind of sport is this? This has got to be the most stupid sport ever! If that was not enough, some of these kids were faster than me. No ball or person was coming to tackle you. You could not possibly get hurt. Well, okay, if you fell on that stick maybe you could get hurt. These guys are sissies. If they weren't sissies, they would be playing football or baseball!

We did have one ace in the hole, Todd Fix. No one in any school was this fast. We had a four man relay race. I think that's what they called it. One of our guys fell down and dropped the baton, you know, the stick. By the time they gave the stick to our anchor, Todd, we were 30 yards back. No matter, Todd beat the pack. He had a coke and a few hot dogs before the rest of the field crossed the line. Well, I might have exaggerated a little, but we did win.

Running isn't a sport because anybody can do it…if you can't get hurt, it is not a sport.

- George Carlin

Baseball

I do believe that Sister Thomas said it best when she asked me if the way to heaven was through baseball. My mind wandered off on one of its little trips to nowhere. I wanted to tell her that this was our heaven and this was her hell. The sheer pleasure of watching her face twisting into contortions, crying to the heavens, falling to her knees as the men in white jackets would take Sister Tommy-gun away to some padded room, forever.

"This already is heaven, Sister," I smiled a wink at her.

Sorry, I used to have these little fantasies. They call it ADD today. Isn't that just another bunch of crap? We are all one boring speaker away from ADD, aren't we? I still go off on these little tangents, like now for example, anyway, let's get back to baseball. If you had a new glove, you worked it. You pounded a ball into the pocket every day. You soaked it in neatsfoot oil and tied it with a belt or a rope overnight. The process was repeated, but every time you picked it up it went right to your nose. The smell of leather from the glove and the rawhide from the ball could only be matched by those blue mimeograph test papers at school.

We watched the games on TV and we played it every waking hour. We'd find a suitable piece of land, clear the debris, fill in the holes, mow the grass and even build a backstop. You pitched and batted, chose up teams and played until dark or until your mom called you. We'd pay our respects to the field by making sure that it was never empty and it loved us right back.

We collected, gambled and traded the baseball cards and then, unfortunately, we would throw them out. After all, who wants last year's Mickey Mantle when I have this year's? We all had our heroes. Mickey Mantle was mine and I wanted to be just like him.

Willie Mays was a favorite of some, but he had once said that he was better than Mickey. Willie Mays, who made fantastic catches on routine fly balls; fly balls that Mickey's speed would allow him to stand under and pound his glove twice while he waited for it. I put Willie Mays' cards on the sprocket of my brother, Timmy's bike. The spokes of the bike would thrash Willie and sound like a motorcycle. 'Say hey' to that Willie. Never step on a boy's hero.

We did play football too, but only when it was too cold to play baseball. No one traded football cards. It wasn't as big then. Long Island was baseball territory at least until a kid named Boomer[6] grew up. But that's the way it was until the girls showed us a new sport.

---

[6] Norman Julius "Boomer" Esiason (born April 17, 1961) is a former American football quarterback and current network color commentator. He grew up on Long Island.

Lesson 5: The Early Years

Mr. Hand

Maybe, it is best to go back a little before it all started. Please, let's not get weird thoughts about the title. This is an innocent story about a three-year old. Let's call it a foundation of family values and the structure of the household. The stage is set and it is early 1953. We lived in a modest two story white stucco house in the suburbs in Littleton, Long Island, most people called it 'the sticks.' We were on a corner 100 by 100 lot with a garage for a backstop and a long driveway to pitch from. It was the wrong side of the tracks, but we did not know it.

I was a middle child. Before my younger brother was born, my older brother and I shared bunk beds. The room was big enough for two beds, but I guess there was some kind of tradition involved.

The top bunk had a bar that ran across it to make it more difficult for Richie to get in and out. I did not have one. This made no sense to me since I was more likely to fall out than he was. He was eight, which meant he got the top bunk. The top bunk was ironically safer in other ways like an involuntary bladder release. My older sister had her own room and I felt sorry for her. What fun is that?

Our room was never totally dark. I don't know if it was the street lights or some perpetual moon beam. After the lights went out I could still see a fair part of the room. On one boring, nondescript night when we were in bed far too early for our liking, I saw a hand. It was moving down the wall from above. It stopped half-way down the wall and then it spoke to me.

"Hello, Wade."

Its face was clenched in a fist and only the thumb mouthed the words.

"Who are you?" I played along, humoring my brother Richie. I felt pretty stupid talking to his hand, but after all, what else did I have to do?

"I am Mr. Hand," my brother, I mean, Mr. Hand replied.

"Oh, hi Mr. Hand" wondering where this was going.

Mr. Hand, disguised as my brother's fist, continued to entertain me with great stories of the adventures of Mr. Hand, himself (as the Irish say). He would tell me of great baseball players and I would listen until I fell asleep. I felt pretty cool about it and my brother had great stories and he knew how to tell them. This went on for quite some time. Some years later, we made a fourth bedroom and Richie moved into it. But not before my brother Timmy was about two or so. Once again, I shared my room. I moved up to the top bunk. Now my younger brother Timmy was below me for *my* own safety.

When Timmy got to about 3 years old, I took a lesson from Richie and I decided to entertain my little brother. I slipped my hand down the wall, clenched my fist and positioned my thumb as I had practiced so many times for this very moment. I practiced all my stories as well. This was going to be great!

"Hi, Timmy," as I moved my thumb knuckle deftly up and down.

Timmy looked up and said, "I'm not talking to your hand! What do you think I am, stupid?!"

Kindergarten – Mrs. Meyer

As I walked with my mom, I was silent. I was taking in the surroundings. The inside of the school smelled musty, like old books and over-waxed wood floors. There was a big sturdy looking wide stairway with a long banister for sliding.

The nuns came to greet us. They dressed odd and smelled of scorched linen, like our tablecloth after it was recently ironed. I stayed close to my mom as we walked. My older brother and sister had worn this trail before me. This was an essential foundation of my survival on the road ahead of me. I figured if they could do it, I could. We stayed on the main floor as we walked toward the first room on the left by the giant staircase. The nuns already knew my mom and asked her to put me at one of the desks.

The desks were old wooden single units with a table built in that lifted so you could hide stuff from the teacher. I sat down and leaned my head down. The desks had a funny odor, so I licked it.

"Yuck. Yep, that's what it smelled like." Not sure why I did stuff like that. It was an uncontrollable curiosity. I have some more disgusting stories like that, but I'll save you from those for now. The room seemed crowded. Each desk had a kid in it with their mom bent at the waist. They hovered to tell their child to behave for some reason or a threat to be named later. I remember my mom telling me to be good and that she would see me later. I would miss her, but right now I was in awe of all of the kids. There were more kids my size than I had ever seen in one place.

Mrs. Meyer was a kind lady. She dressed like my mom, but she was thinner. She was a little bit older than her years. Kids will do that. She had dark wavy hair and brown eyes that popped out to see behind her when she wrote on the blackboard. Her hands, already covered in white chalk dust, would find her hips when she was mad, which was not often.

Her shoes were also a bit pointier than they should be, as was her nose. She had a constant smile and she would gently hold your face in her hands when needed. If she were really from Oz, she would have been one of the nice ones from the North or the South.

Confessions of an Altar Boy

I had Mrs. Meyer in kindergarten and again in 3rd grade. She and my mom were friends and I had been at her house many times. I had to be on my best behavior even with the substitute teacher. My mother would take Mrs. Meyer's place whenever she was out. I could not wait for fourth grade so I could get my punishment only once and stay after with the big boys. I was sitting there on my first day taking in the surroundings when another interesting odor came drifting by. It was more disgusting than interesting, so I checked my pants, "Nope, not me." I looked around and right there under this kid Joey's seat was a poop on the floor, make that two and a half poops. This bothered me because Joey was already five. Would this happen to me at five?

At this age, I figured I would be beyond a crisis of that nature. Anyway, I pointed this out to Mrs. Meyer. Later on at recess, I learned my first lesson about not telling on anyone.

I wasn't four. I was four and a half as we used to put it. I started very early and I was younger than most of the kids. Platinum blonde hair and blue eyes like cornflowers as my mom would say. Mom could say that, but a guy could get beat up for saying something like that. My cheeks always had color even when there wasn't any dirt on them. My dad and my brother told me not to take any crap from anyone. So, I would have a black eye or a fat lip to complete my school picture each year.

Richie was five years ahead of me. He was one of the big kids. He was huge. He was at least four feet something, maybe more! He had brown hair, blue eyes and muscles on his muscles. He lifted weights, played baseball and he could beat up anybody that I knew, so nobody messed with him. I tried to use him as leverage.

"Fight your own battles," he would say.

I wished he had told me that before I smart-mouthed Lenny, the neighborhood bully. You learn a lot of important lessons when you are four and a half. It was probably for the best. Richie would graduate way before me and then I would have five more years to fend for myself.

Girl Crazy

We had a great neighborhood that had all the creature comforts any kid would want. We had a homegrown baseball field that my brother and all our friends had built. We had more than enough kids in the ten blocks to field any sport. We were surrounded by woods and streams. You could start up any type of game or trouble your hearts desired. Let's make that *mild* trouble, as our parents knew everywhere we went and everything we did. We had no problem with the concept that God sees everything.

"Heck, my Mom can do that."

We had railroad tracks, a luncheonette, a deli and even a beer and soda place within walking distance. All of the storekeepers and all of the parents knew who we were. There was no need for cell phones or a tracking system, they had party lines. And we had something else that is pretty rare in today's market, we had respect. Respect that can best be defined this way: if I ever did anything to embarrass my parents, I would get the ever loving crap beat out of me. That was pretty much the rule of thumb in the 50s.

When I was about four, a family moved in down the street. There was an older kid named Charlie and his sister Valerie. Charlie was two years older than me and that alone would have made him very cool, but he was also from Brooklyn.

I had never heard anyone talk like that.

"Wanna play baseball today, *Wade*?!"

All of the words seemed to rise in tone with the accent on the last word, my name. It made everything sound more important, more urgent. It made you pay attention. It was as if the accent was not on the last syllable but on the very last word of any sentence. How cool is that? I tried it many times, but you can't fake Brooklyn.

Charlie was good at baseball. He was good at everything. He taught us the importance of ring-a-levio, but more about that later. More importantly, he had a sister. She was closer to my age. Back then, Valerie had a mountain of blonde hair that the wind would often use to hide those brown eyes, eyes that could make you forget what you were saying. She was a bit younger than me and off the baseball field, I spent every daylight hour over her house.

Her yard was fenced in and she was too young to roam like someone as old and worldly as I was. I would tell her of great adventures outside those walls. They were mostly true. After all, I could not lie, not to her. For a time, that fence surrounded our world in its safe hands.

We would play card games like go-fish or some board game. We'd always make up our own rules because we did not know how to play until Charlie showed us. He would walk away feeling some gratification that he had taught us the right way.

"I liked it better the way we did it," Valerie would say after he left.

"Yeah, this is boring." We'd put the cards away and find something else to do the wrong way.

We would pretend to be the people that we saw on television, mostly cartoon characters. The people on TV did things like Charlie, but the cartoon characters did things the way we liked to do them.

When it started to get colder, the days became shorter and so did our time together. We'd stretch it. It started to get dark before dinner now. We would sit on the cement porch. It should have been cold, but kids never notice the cold until their parents tell them.

"Do you want to catch a cold?"

"Come in and get your jacket."

"In or out. Do you live in a barn?"

Without realizing it, I would store these sayings away. Later in life, I too would blurt them out to my children and walk away shaking my head in shameful resignation. This is called ATS (Adult Tourette's Syndrome).

We'd look up at the moon and wonder about us. We would talk about the characters that we had invented and wonder what was real. I knew what was real, but I could not find the words. That was, until Valentine's Day. I wanted to buy her one of those cards. I was at the store with my mom and I asked her.

"I want to get one of these for Valerie."

Mom thought it was cute, but then insulted me by casually laughing about something called 'puppy love' with the store clerk. We got the card though and that's all that mattered. I struggled to write something on the card. It might have been easier for me had I known that this is something that haunted all men for eternity: How to make a girl happy? What to say,

'Something beautiful for my something beautiful.'

You're kidding me, right? I could hardly write my name much less say something as poetic as that.

I could not do much without my mom's help. So, no, I did not come up with something as spectacular as that. We put her name on the top and mine at the bottom. Ironically, Valerie was not even four. She could not read yet anyway. I put the card in the envelope, sealed it and stuck it under my pillow. I did not want my brother to find it or even know about it. I was sure he would muster more than mom's two words with a dash of harassment from his arsenal of fun. There were rules. *If it is not a baseball card, then it isn't cool.*

Anyway, it was February 13th. I remember that I could not sleep that night. All I could think about was her and that wonderful card. I was thinking about tomorrow and why my stomach hurt? I could still hear my mom giggling. Puppy love?! I don' think so! I'll run off with her, and we'll get married, and then they'll be sorry! Finally, exhaustion got the best of me. I awoke the next morning, but then panicked as the card was gone.

I bet Richie took it. I bet he and Julie are laughing as they read it in her room! I panicked as I scrambled around the mattress.

"Ah, I found it."

It had fallen behind the bed and not into their hands. It would not escape me again. It went with me until the time of delivery. I am sure my fingerprints are still embossed on that envelope somewhere. I cleaned up, got dressed, brushed my teeth, faked eating a bowl of Sugar-Pops and I went off with card in hand down the block. I was early.

Valerie was still eating breakfast, so I waited for her outside. Her mom had some Valentine candies and made us promise not to eat any before lunch. Valerie gave me some and I gave her the card. She spun the envelope around in her hands like a toy and held it up to the light.

She said, "What's this?"

"It's a card," I said a bit over anxiously, "Open it."

She ripped it open and stared at the card like you would a sandwich to see what kind of meat was in it. "What does it say?"

"It says 'Be my Valentine'."

"Oh. Okay," she said matter-of-factly, and then we played.

As I walked home that day, I said, "I have a girlfriend!"

I'm not sure Valerie looked at that way. I told my mom that Valerie was my girlfriend and she repeated those two words. Now I was getting mad.

"That's it! Tomorrow, we are definitely running off together!!" was all I could muster in my angry thoughts.

Well, it seemed pretty real to me! Later on in life, my mom would piss me off with two other words, 'Girl Crazy.' She was right about a lot of things and she got even smarter as I got older.

School Sisters of Our Lady

The first nun that you ever see is a bit of a shock, at least back in the 50's. Today you can't tell one from a businesswoman with very little money.

All nuns are married to Christ. Anyone who has seen the "Bells of Saint Mary's" has a pretty good picture and an idea of their devotion. I have no doubt in their faith, as I have no doubt in their diligence to perform their duties. But they are as diverse in their methods and in their delivery, as they are in their personalities. They are just like anyone else in this world. When I was very young, I asked, "Sister? How come you became a nun?

She simply said, "Because I had the calling."

"We have a lot of that in my neighborhood too," I said.

Kids can be pretty cruel, I thought as I walked away. Maybe I should be more careful what I call my sister from now on. There is a hierarchy among the nuns. There is an order and a reverence about them. Still, there is something mysterious wrapped in their minds perhaps by the garments they wore, something that could not be easily read. As time went by, I felt that they did not so much wear the habit as much as they were hiding safely behind it.

My first impression of a nun is like no other.

1ˢᵗ Grade - Sister Mary Lynn

I am five years old.

"Hey, I am five-and-a-half, thank you!"

I stand about three-foot-nothing and here she comes with a bit of a happy lilt to her brisk pace. There is no visible hair except the eyebrows, no neck and no ears. The only part showing is her face, framed in pure white cloth. All are then shrouded in a black cotton curtain that runs from the top of her head to the top of her black-laced shoes. A string of black beads with a crucifix held by small silver links was her only accessory.

Below a starched white band is a mere part of her forehead and her eyebrows are the only clue to the color of her hair. Her eyes, her nose, and her chin, are her only identifying features. Her name is Sister Mary Lynn. The mention of her name gives me pause even now.

She is young, too young for the task. She smiles too often for the order of things and she is absolutely, positively beautiful. She is a thinner version of Ingrid Bergman but no less beautiful. I imagined under all of that cloth she had blonde hair to match those summer sky baby blues. Todd, Dylan and I were more than secretly in love with her. All the boys were. If you even thought of the word penguin, we'd kill you.

After a few years, Dylan and I summoned up the courage to tell Sister Mary Lynn that she was too beautiful to be a nun. For some reason, she did not take this as a compliment. She made us clean the floor and the desks with a toothbrush and gave us a lecture on something called vanity. Yeah, right. We got to stay after school with her. I still think she was flattered as I caught a little smile while we worked.

Having missed the opportunity, Todd tried to tell her the same thing the next day, but she was wise to us by then.

Imagine our surprise when we met the rest of the nuns. To give you a point of reference, it would be like going from one of Kennedy's girl friends to one of Bill Clinton's. No, that is too kind. I gave this some thought. I still didn't get it. I could see why the other nuns took this path. They were either heavy, or they were too old to get married. We did not imagine that they ever had a younger existence before we met them.

Nicknames were common. Sister Agnes was Prune Face. Sister Thomas was Tommy-gun or the great Stone-face. The nuns we liked never had nicknames. Remember love: respect, fear: nickname. These little things are important if you want to communicate and survive recess.

The nuns were our teachers, our guides on trips and our coaches in many sports. They were masters of 'the look.' One has to imagine that since all Italians are Catholics, the Mafia 'look' was born from a parochial education. The sisters had a flawless backhand. They could belittle you with an ear pull or scar you for life in front of your friends. These were the School Sisters of Our Lady. They were a force to be reckoned with on and off the field.

Interlaced with the nuns were a few teachers that were not nuns. They varied like the nuns in size and attractiveness. Mrs. Winters was pretty hot. They were called Lay-teachers. We couldn't say those words without snickering. Laughter was not allowed. Remember?

The teachers were all woman and the bus drivers were all men. The world had a certain order to it and we liked it that way. I do remember our first female bus driver. It was in our last year at St. Mary's. I am not sure if she was odd, the concept was more than odd to us. It was unsettling. We were the only ones with a woman bus driver. We'd arrive at school the same time as the other buses. We might as well have worn ear-muffs. As if being a Saint Mary's fairy was not enough to shoulder. We rode our bikes to school a lot that year.

The Polio Epidemic

It was 1955. A disease that had taken so many, including one of our presidents, was still in research. The disease was polio. Each year 57,000 more were infected with this disease. So little was known, but there was one shining light, the Jonas Salk[7] vaccine. It was not a proven vaccine, but they could wait no longer, something must be done. Some kids would get the vaccine and the others, a placebo injection.

We were sitting in first grade waiting for our turn. We had heard about these giant foot long needles that were an inch thick. They were going to stick us with them three times, hard! We knew that because the second graders went before recess and they told us all about it. Then they would snicker. We had not mastered the snicker yet, so we did not know what it meant.

There was total silence as a deep, loud knock was heard and then the classroom door opened.

"Sister Mary Lynn, please bring your class downstairs."

I felt some kind of burning in my chest and throat and I was shaking. I was not alone. We wobbled two-by-two downstairs on those shaky knees and with sweaty palms. We could see two stations with a uniformed nurse and a white-jacketed doctor at each. The word, 'next.' was not

---

[7] **Jonas Salk** (October 28, 1914 – June 23, 1995) was an American medical researcher and virologist, best known for his discovery and development of the first safe and effective polio vaccine.

necessary, as the mere sound of 'ouch!' was all that was needed.

Our two-by-two formation became rather sloppy due to the bobbing of heads taking a look and, of course, the occasional fainted-body lying on the floor. Nice try, but that did not work, believe me.

Each of us went to the station ahead of us. They marked our names down in a medical journal. It was only one shot and the needle wasn't all that big. It was tiny compared to the stories. I hate second graders. It still felt it though, and I said, "Ouch." It did not hurt. I only did that so the girl behind me would know that it was her turn.

After we had the shots, we went back to class with Sister Mary Lynn. We kept checking our arms to see why it itched. Then we would scratch it.

"Do not scratch," Sister Mary Lynn would tell us.

"It itches, Sister," we pleaded.

"You will only make it worse."

We would stop for a minute or two and the same sentences would be exchanged again throughout the day.

Day after day that early October, I sat intermingled with those that had the vaccine and those that did not. None of us even knew there was a difference. We had forgotten about the whole needle incident anyway.

Being a five year old, I did not know what was about to happen. Being five I did not know that those who got the vaccine had traces of polio: a living virus. The small amount of virus was used to promote the body's ability to fight the disease, along with the vaccine. I did not know that I was given a placebo and neither did Steven, Maryann or the rest of the half of us. We had no protection and the other half sitting all around us were now carriers of the disease. They had the vaccine, we did not. We were helpless cultures in Petri dishes.

To put this in perspective, sit in front of this class as a teacher. Imagine four rows of five-year-old children, as they stare adoringly at you. Half are protected; half are not. Every other child in the class may be infected at any time: some of these chairs will soon be empty. Picture yourself as a parent with only two children. It may be hard to recollect that far back for some. Others will choose not to remember at all. I remember it all vividly. Every story has a dark chapter that, in life, cannot be skipped over. You may wish to, but stay with me a while.

The Waves

It did not take very long. It was somewhere before Halloween of 1955. I had a costume that I would never wear. I was lying on the couch, burning. I felt a surge of fiery pain rushing from my feet to my head and then back again like water being carried in a long tub. It moved from head to toe, burning my joints with each pass.

Mom's normally warm hand now felt cold as she pressed it against my head. My body was on fire, but my bones were like ice. My skin felt like it would melt and my stomach was a convulsing inferno. The wave came.

It was a protective separation of body from mind and spirit. Survival by divesting yourself from the pain and the body that caused it. I was outside of myself.

The temperature of the body was now over 104 and it tortured this five-year old frame and it tortured his young mind.

"Mommy, please make it stop," he was crying. His body's racking with waves of pain.

I could see my mom holding him close. She told him that it would stop. It was reassuring and he believed her. The waves finally subsided for the moment and he… he… I was back again. I had no thoughts but to have this pain go away. Why won't someone help me?

My mother was a pretty strong person, stronger than my dad, especially emotionally. And then another wave came.

While holding him helplessly in their arms, with their thoughts of what it was and what it could mean, they were ripped apart by what they were seeing in front of them.

The wave went away again. I could see my sister and my brother peeking from the stairway. Julie was 9 and Richie was almost 11 by then. They were a lot older than me, but they looked scared and my sister was in tears. They were not allowed near me. My little brother, Timmy, was only about 8 months old and he was sleeping. He was not allowed near me either.

I drifted away into a much-needed sleep.

I was always playing some form of baseball with Richie in the backyard. We were having a catch and Richie would throw me some ground balls. I did not like them because they would bounce unexpectedly and hit you in the face.

"Get in front of it."

"What are you nuts?!"

"Don't turn your head."

But suddenly I got it, I understood perfectly. One after another came and I would snatch them up like a pro. I grabbed one backhanded and snapped the ball back to Richie. Hey, this is my dream.

I was thinking of asking Richie if….but then the waves came again, and I woke up abruptly.

The family doctor's name was Doctor Candy. He came to the house and examined him. The doctor was a very well-dressed and distinguished, dark haired man with a tool he stuck in his ears as he listened to the boy's chest.

The wave passed. There was something very comforting about his way and he even made the pain listen as he spoke. Doctors have more comforting power than they know. I liked him and wondered why he was named after my favorite food group.

He did not smell like candy, he smelled like soap. I was amazed how good I felt after the waves would pass. It was like I was not sick at all. I felt weak.

I told him exactly what I had felt. I told him about the waves and that they were stronger now. With the temperature and his other instruments, he confirmed that it was polio. My mother fell to her knees as my dad hugged me like he had never hugged me before. Even Dr. Candy hugged me. He drove us to Saint Charles Hospital that very night. And then the wave came back sooner and stronger than ever before.

I must have thankfully passed out along the way. I woke up with intravenous bags of Salk and saline attached to my calves, thighs, forearms, upper arms and even my stomach. I could feel them pinching me, but they did not hurt. I could not feel much of anything.

It is still that same night. I am in shock and I can feel nothing. I see the pain on my Mom's face. To my surprise, I could still talk, "Hi Mommy." I told her that I felt better and asked her if we could go home now. She said, "We'll see," but she knew better and somehow, so did I. And then the waves came and as the Salk vaccine took effect, this would be for the last time. When it subsided, I went into a deep and well-needed sleep. Good dreams are an essential part of the healing process.

I dreamed of baseball again and this time the whole family was playing, even my little brother, Timmy, our eight-month-old catcher.

The Morning After

I had a bed like this a few years back when I had my tonsils out. I was thinking of this as I woke up. I hope they bring ice cream. That's what you get to eat when you are in the hospital, I remembered. The bed had rails on both sides like Timmy's crib. I still had a few needles with tubes but not as many. I could see forever in this long ward and there were beds everywhere, maybe 30 or more with a kid in each one. Every single one of them had polio. The kid next to me said his name was Mark, and that he went to St. Mary's school.

"I know Mark. I am in St. Mary's too," I said.

He could not seem to remember. He was in second grade so why would he. We talked about the waves. He still had them and he had lots of tubes. I told him I haven't had any more waves since last night.

"I think those tubes will stop yours too."

Mark went to sleep again.

"Hey, wait a minute, no more waves! Hey, where's my Mom?"

But there was some throbbing in my legs and lower back that was not nearly as bad as those waves. I did not care. I wanted to see Mom and Dad, NOW!!

There were nuns everywhere who were actually our nurses. They had white and gray habits and smiled when they talked to you, but they still wouldn't bring you ice cream even when you played the "*but I'm so sick*" routine.

It must have been in the wee hours of the morning when Dr. Candy drove my parents back home. The babysitter must have spent the night at our house. It was late morning before my Mom got back to Saint Charles.

"Hi sweetheart, how do you feel?"

"I feel great, Mom, can I go home now?" Mark said it would not work, but I figured that I would give it a shot.

"No, honey, you'll need to stay a while longer."

I broke down and cried right in front of Mark and everyone. She would not take me home and I did not understand. Mark was older. He told me that we were sick and we could make others sick, so we needed to stay until we were better. It helped a little but not really. I was selfish and did not care about those who did not hurt.

Mark told me a joke. I didn't get it, but I laughed anyway. I did that a lot when I watched people like Milton Berle. I gave a good laugh and Mark started to laugh and we felt pretty good. Mark showed me how to play a card game called War. It helped pass the time and sometimes he'd let me win.

The medicine was helping, but Mark's waves would not go away and then he had another bad one.

"Sister! Nurse!" I yelled and they came to fix the tubes. They held Mark as they said the Hail Mary and he went into a grateful sleep again.

In the weeks that followed, the pain went away, but so did my ability to walk. I could not feel my legs at all and they said that my spine was curved. Mark's waves spread out a lot more, but they would not go away. He was in more pain than I was, but he was very brave and did not complain like me. After a wave, Mark would go to sleep. I knew how good it felt to sleep. I did not disturb him. One day Mark kept on sleeping and they took him away. They told me that he went home. I missed Mark, as he was my strength. He did not say goodbye before he left and I tried not to think about what that meant. You would be amazed at what a five-year old can block out and amazed at what he knows. I said a prayer for Mark that night and whenever I remember.

If She Could, I Could

I met other placebo classmates at Saint Charles as well. Mary Ann seemed in better shape than me. She was walking with some assistance. When I saw her, I knew that I would get better too. One thing for sure, I wanted to play baseball with my brother again: Richie that is. Okay and Timmy too. I can teach him when he gets older.

My mom came every day and my dad came on weekends. It seemed like forever and I had only been there for 5 weeks. My parents were allowed to bring me home for Thanksgiving since I was free of any polio. I was left with its angry signature. I still could not walk, but I was better and I was alive. It was nice to be home for Thanksgiving, but it was torture as they had to bring me back the next day. I began to understand the emotional and physical pain and saw little difference between the two.

I started to feel my legs again and had to tell them to stop sticking pins in my feet. The hospital had constructed a back brace for me and I was doing exercises to help strengthen my back and my legs. I could feel my legs and my toes, and after a few weeks, I could walk with braces! My parents had thought that I would never walk again. I did not think of it that way. I never thought of it that way. I saw kids in wheelchairs and thought they were not ready yet. I see them today, and I think of what could have been.

Once I could walk without the braces, I would sneak over to the girl's side. Mary Ann was going home. I was jealous and I would miss her. She was the only girl I could talk to. After the nuns in the hospital could not catch me anymore they sent me home for Christmas and for good. The nuns at St. Charles were kind. They never punished me even if I was bad. Later I would find the horrible reality, not all nuns are like Sister Mary Lynn and the ones at St. Charles.

My exodus from the hospital was eventful as my whole family came. I would never see any of those kind hospital nuns again. They were so happy.

I would come back every week or so for a while but only to have x-rays and see the doctor. He would tell me how well I was doing and how lucky I was.

"Lucky? How about I stick you with a placebo!"

By Christmas Day 1955, I had no limp, no pain and I was running. In my mind, I ran faster than I had ever run before. I still wore the back brace and walked pretty stiff. Grandma told me that I walked like a soldier.

When January came, it was hard to go back to school. The brace made sitting at the desk intolerable. Part of it may have been that I could not catch up on the 3 months that I had missed. More importantly, I made some of the ignorant parents of the other children nervous. They did not want their kids near me. My mom decided to keep me home the rest of that year. I went back to first grade in '56. By then I shed the brace and no one could tell I ever had polio.

Because of polio, I grew no taller that year, but I had grown up a lot inside. I learned about life and death. I had no doubts accepting that there is a life afterward. I had experienced the separation of body and spirit. I knew more than any five-year old should know. Naturally, I had to go back to first grade and Sister Mary Lynn gave me this huge hug and cried when she saw me. I hugged her back and did not want to let go.

"You're in my class," she said, holding me by the shoulders at arm's length with a huge smile.

"I know, Sister."

I was beaming too. You see? After all, I loved this beautiful person who happened to be a nun. I was closer in age to the kids in my class now. I was thankful, as I felt more in place here than with the kids that were now in second grade. Life would have been very different, so maybe polio gave me as much as it had taken.

I breezed through first grade and did not realize that meant I would not have Sister Mary Lynn again the next year.

Lesson 6: The Conjunction of 3 M

2nd Grade – Sister Alice

I have no vivid memories of Sister Alice. She was nice and all, but she was Agnes Moorhead next to the Ingrid Bergman beauty of Sister Mary Lynn. She would have been one of the older nuns you did not notice in the *Bells of St. Mary's*[8]. One of life's lessons is the effect of a woman's beauty on a young man's memory, actually any person's memory. I remember that she was more strict than Sister Mary Lynn. There was a touch of gray about her eyes. She was lean and she was neat as the proverbial pin. She was taller and gave a lot of tests.

We were seven, at most. It is in this class that I met my two subversive friends forever, Todd and Dylan.

---

[8] ***The Bells of St. Mary's*** (1945) Rainbow Productions - American film tells the story of a priest and a nun who set out, despite their good-natured rivalry, to save a school. Starring Ingrid Bergman and Bing Crosby.

The Conjunction

Dylan was the oldest being born in January. Dylan was thin, dark-haired with freckles and did not like any reference to Alfalfa as I found out at the bus stop one day. He was tall and the girls giggled whenever he walked by. They loved him and this problem would haunt him forever.

Todd was younger than Dylan by eight months. Still, he made up for it with his size. He was bigger and broader. Only Todd and I had the blonde hair, but blue eyes were common for the three of us. No cornflower references, please. The girls were crazy about Todd and me too, but they would wait a few years to tell us this. *(Aside: Hey, it's my story.)*

My life would not have been the same and I would not be the same person today without these guys. Remember this: parents may guide, but your friends influence your behavior. This is what molds the shape of your life.

Todd lived about five blocks from me. He had a big yard and our mothers were friends. They were housewives, which meant they were home all day. Parents did not worry about their kids getting kidnapped or poisoned. They didn't worry about drugs. We could roam for ten blocks and not go anywhere anonymously, not even downtown. A spanking was only a phone call away. We told them where we would be, but they already knew.

Confessions of an Altar Boy

They could recount our every move with a party line[9], which was the LoJack[10] of the times. Dylan was from Brooklyn. He and his parents had moved a lot before finally settling into Littleton. He was only a block from Todd and we hoped his parents would stay put this time. We spent seven days a week with each other mostly at school or the baseball field that was built by us, the neighborhood kids.

Our separate paths converged in second grade. This was the great conjunction. For us to end up in the same class, fell somewhere in the realm of divine providence and alphabetical destiny. The nuns had other terms for this fate that had befallen upon them.

We shoveled snow, raked leaves, delivered papers, played little league and joined the scouts before we moved on to high school. If it was not enough that we were Maguire, McBurke and Morgan, we all had younger brothers the same age. They could now bother each other and leave us alone. After all, with pompous pride, it was up to us to make a path for them to follow. Or since no one is totally useless, we could always serve as a bad example and they could choose - not to follow.

---

[9] Party line: In twentieth century telephone systems, a party line (also multiparty line or Shared Service Line) is an arrangement in which two or more customers are connected directly to the same local loop.

[10] LoJack: A System used in conjunction with law enforcement agencies for the recovery of stolen vehicles.

The Conjunction

Our classroom was on the first floor on the back corner of that same old building. There were lots of windows on two sides and we could see anyone walking in the play area. It was not distracting because the entire building went to recess at the same time. It was annoying because everything we did at recess could be seen from those windows; a point that had escaped me one beautiful spring day.

Baseball cards were a big item then. You could buy five cards and get a stick of bubble gun for five cents. We would use our skill by flipping them end over end.

"Heads! I win! Tails you lose!" would be shouted at random as the game was decided.

For us, these expressions were born here. You flipped the card by gently holding it in the tips of your fingers and thumb. You held the card close to your side and parallel to the ground. Then you would move your arm slowly backward and then slowly forward, letting the card slip off your thumb which caused the card to flip end over end. You had to match the card that was thrown. If you did, then you would win both cards, if you did not, you lost.

It was simple and fair. Sometimes there were up to five cards that you had to match. I was pretty good at it and I had won a lot that day before getting back into class.

"That's gambling young man! I want you to return all of those cards right now!"

"Yes, sister."

Confessions of an Altar Boy

I had to go around the class and each person had to announce how many cards they had lost to me. By the time I finished, I had fewer cards than when I had started. Well, so much for their Christian upbringing.

My fondest recollection of Sister Alice is that this was the only time she would ever catch…scold me. I do remember that she had the most perfect handwriting and I also remember that we did not. It was her job to teach us. Handwriting was an actual subject. There was this perfectly annoying banner that sprawled across the highest point of the walls of the room with these perfect capital and perfect small letters that made me perfectly sick to look at them.

The ballpoint pen was invented in 1935 and managed to hit the shelves in 1945. Here we were, more than ten years later, and we were not allowed to use them. Apparently, ballpoint pens were invented by a Protestant or a Jew, so we had to use a *fountain pen* until a Catholic invented one. We did not have cartridges, we had ink wells right there in the desk with jars of ink in them.

The instructions were pretty straightforward:

You unscrew the top of the bottle, place the fountain pen, nib (the point) first, into the bottle until the nib is entirely covered in ink, then press the metal bar to deflate the bladder and slowly release the metal bar to fill the bladder. Remove the nib from the ink and gently blot the excess from the nib, your shirt, the desk, your lunch and your trousers.

We are now ready to write in the Palmer Method[11]. We are all now ready to copy those freakin' perfect symbols from the wall. Sister Alice would say, "Capital A," and we would write that down and then she would say "capital B," as we were finished with our version of capital A.

I snuck a peek over at poor Todd, as his left-handedness would trail behind, sweeping an inexcusable smudge across what he'd just written. Dylan and I, being right-handed did not have to wait for each letter to dry before writing the next. You would keep little tidbits like this, which we called ammunition. In case you want to make fun of someone later on, ammunition is the key. So with knowledge way beyond my years and being older, I said to Todd, "You're using the wrong hand!"

Then I evaluated Todd's reaction along with the physical size of him and added, "But it looked pretty good before you smudged it."

We wrote everything down in composition books in order to preserve our work. I sincerely felt that the three of us would be famous someday and people would want these as collectibles.

A composition or copybook, as we called it, had a black and white marble cardboard cover with a white box where you could write your name and the subject. When you opened it each page had blue horizontal lines that

---

[11] The Palmer Method of penmanship instruction was developed and promoted by Austin Palmer in the early 1900s. It soon became the most popular handwriting system in the United States.

started about one inch from the top. Every page had a red line that ran down the left-hand side. This red line was one inch from the left border. All were designed to show the teacher how far off the mark you wrote your letters.

There was something patriotic in its look and feel. Getting a brand new copybook was very cool. We wrote our names neatly on the front. Once opened, it was not possible to write twenty-six letters without spilling some ink. With a fountain pen, this was our destiny. Every school in the diocese was taught this way, perhaps every diocese in the world was equally tortured.

In a few years, a Catholic finally reinvented the ballpoint pen and rescued us from these weapons of mass instruction.

Sister Agnes – A Matter of Principal

They say she sang in the opera. We wished that she had stayed there. Her punishments were ruthless and if it wasn't a corporal punch, it would be worse. She would pull on your ear and make you kneel, belittling and scarring you for life in front of your friends. She was small but tall enough, she was thin but strong enough, she was wrinkled, far more than enough and we made fun of her in her absence. She was our principal. Her name, in front of her face, was Sister Agnes.

She replaced Sister Lawrence, the antithesis of Agnes. Sister Lawrence was warm. She smiled and we welcomed her visits to the classroom. I had a good *in* with her as my brother Richie already won her favor. She would always ask me how he was doing at St. Anthony's.

Richie had gone on to a Catholic high school, kind of a self-flagellation thing. I guess Richie wanted to see if the brothers of St. Anthony's could smack you around harder than a nun. Richie would answer that with a definitive 'yes!'

Getting back to my answer, "Just fine, Sister," I said. Sister Lawrence's warm smile reminded me of my grandmother.

But then she left and we ended up with the unmasked *Tantrum of the Opera*. As we moved into our brand new school, we left a lot of the warmth of that old building in too many ways.

We had mixed emotions about the brand new desks too. The tops did not move and there was no place to hide your stuff. They had a shelf under your seat but no inkwells.

Everything was new, even most of the textbooks. The walls were all freshly painted a light green. The floors were no longer wooden. They looked like they were made of tiny tan pebbles, but it was smooth as glass to the touch. You could see through the stone-like steps of the stairways, a major design flaw. We moved into this beautiful new school finely chilled by her very icy omnipotent and eerie presence. We entered into these new surroundings and the third grade.

3rd Grade - Mrs. Meyer

My mother's friend was my 3rd-grade teacher. "What could be worse?" you ask.

Well at times going to school is like preparing for battle. "I have met the substitute teacher and she is my mother."

Could it be worse? I guess your mother being a nun would be worse, but that's not possible, is it? I'll tell you what it is like. It is like getting your report card every doggone day! All of the habitual nonsense we did to the teachers must stop when your mom is up there. Well, at least for you, it does. For your friends, it is an opportunity to pull the teacher's chain and yours at the same time. Then at recess, you can kick the crap out of the kid who harassed your mom. After that, you and your mom can go down to the principal's office in single file. This is what we call a lose-lose situation because later that day dad gets to hear the whole story too. How many times can a kid get spanked for protecting his mom's honor?

The answer is *none!* All I got was a mild lecture from, as Yogi Berra would put it, "from both of the three of them."

This is where I learned the fuzzy logic between nearly right and almost wrong. Or in the fifties what we called, "What did you say about my mother!?"

The Cold War

The Cold War was named after the rift between the students and Sister Agnes. Later on, the term was stolen to describe the relationship between Russia and the United States. Dwight D. Eisenhower was our president and he wanted us to be prepared in case of a nuclear attack. He was a pretty cool president.

Dad said. "You know, he's a general, so he really knows what he is talking about."

Mom said, "He's a golfer, and the country runs better when he stays on the course."

But President Eisenhower could even pronounce the challenging word *nuclear*, a lost art for our politicians of today. My father said he was a Republican and that seemed to be as important to Dad. I kept pronouncing *nuclear* until I got it right.

We had air-raid drills to make sure we knew how to kneel under our desks. These brand new flimsy desks were going to protect us as long as we were underneath them (as worthwhile as having your seatback in the upright position in case of a 500 mph airplane crash). Even public schools did this, but Catholics are expert kneelers, so we already had a leg up on everyone. Had this been a real emergency, however, I would have ducked under a nun's habit. You can bet nothing is getting under there. Drills seemed pretty frequent. If it wasn't an air raid, it was a fire drill.

Confessions of an Altar Boy

In case of a fire, we would line up outside of our classroom in a two by two formation. The trick here is to take the side by the wall when you pair up. In case of a real fire, you can use the outside kid as a shield.

We would wait until the entire class was assembled. They would rather lose all of us than only one of us. We would then proceed to the nearest stairwell, walk down and wait outside. Air raids were held on sunny days: fire drills were held on cold rainy days because of the sin of enjoyment.

This was a good time to sharpen our *whisper, snicker and giggle* routines. The girls giggled and the boys snickered. The nuns slapped us for not paying attention, which was part of *their* practice. After each of us had enough of honing our parochial skills we went back inside.

I can't remember ever thinking about a real bomb. I never imagined climbing out of the tons of rubble that my plywood desk had protected me from. I saw pictures of mushroom clouds on the television and they were cool. Maybe I did not see enough pictures of the aftermath. If I had, I would have stored my baseball glove more carefully or brought it with me.

It was a terrible time for parents. They seemed to worry about every little thing. Valerie and Charlie's parents built an air-raid shelter in their basement. They kept it a secret by telling everybody, one person at a time.

Paranoia and fear ran abreast. They even had a Twilight Zone[12] episode about it. In the story, the siren went off with no warning and the neighbors almost killed the only people who had a shelter. Valerie had nothing to worry about; I would have protected her once they let me in.

Kids are resilient. The drills scarred us so deeply that by the time the bus came that afternoon, we talked about baseball. "Oh, that is a defense mechanism," a therapist would say.

I am sure that, today, parents would be concerned about the psychological damage that an air-raid drill might yield on a young child. Don't you love those over-doting parental types? All I can say to them is "Kiss my ass you Doctor Spock-following, sissy-raising, spine-removing, pussy-footers! That's why your kids are in therapy today."

You can always recognize a therapist or one needing therapy as early as the third grade. He would be the one getting the shit kicked out of him repeatedly during recess. Oh! *Excuse me*! I meant him *or her*.

If you start referring to *repressed thoughts*, "Find yourself a nice splint to straighten your wrists out!" And, I want to thank my parents and all of the teachers for smacking us around (especially, those other kids that deserved it).

---

[12] Twilight Zone was a popular TV Series (1959-64) created by Rod Serling they were a mixture of 30 minute self-contained fantasy, science fiction and suspense stories.

It is a tough world out there. All of the top executives and successful people I know today go to only one type of therapist and that's for a deep tissue massage.

Confessions on a Hot Cross Bun

There were a lot of hard ways to get to heaven. If you followed all of the commandments, prayed a lot and were nice to people all of the time without exception, you *might* make it to heaven. Certainly most of the nuns would fail number three, but somehow they already had an 'in.' There were other ways and other avenues to that stairway.

There was this other promise that you would go to heaven if you went to mass and received Holy Communion for nine consecutive first Fridays. I am not sure how this works because this seems too simple to me. This can't be right, being a Catholic and getting to heaven is not all that easy. This needed further investigation, but, hey, who am I to question a gift. We gave it a shot.

As a Catholic, you could not eat before receiving Holy Communion. Since we all had skipped breakfast, the school and the local bakery provided us with buns. Most of the time they were hot cross buns, but once in a while, they were cheese-filled, my favorite. This would be our breakfast along with a half pint of milk that morning.

To be able to take advantage of these great offerings of heaven and the cheese buns, you had to go to confessions. This is where you tell the priest all of the bad things you had done since your last Act of Contrition (confession). It takes place in a confessional.

The confessional is dark. It looks a bit like a wooden phone booth with a thick curtain instead of a door. Once the curtain is closed, it adds darkness and the just the right gloom to the occasion. Your eyes are slow to adjust. There is no seat that I was aware of, only a kneeler that you bang your shins into as you take your station.

It is somehow cold even on the hottest days and the curtain might as well be of metal because it is too late to escape. You've rehearsed this in line a hundred times, but you are nervous and the darkness becomes your friend as you believe it hides your identity. And then you wait.

The priest has his own phone booth that is attached to yours. Right now he is hearing the confession of the poor bastard on the other side. Oops, "bastard?" I'll add one to the count of 'bad words' I must confess.

A little eye-level sliding door revealed that there was only a screen between the two of you. His side is as dark as yours, but this is of little help to him, you already know who *he* is. You are facing him as he sits sideways revealing only a shadowy profile. He does not look at you as you confess your very sinful, once private, life. And so, a true confession goes *meekly* and most of them are something like this:

"Yes, my son?" as he slides the door open.

"Bless me, Father, for I have sinned. My last confession was…uh… one week ago. "

"Yes, my son, please go ahead."

"I fought with my younger brother."

"How many times?"

"About two, Father."

"How many times!?"

"Maybe more like five, Father."

"Yes, and what else, my son?"

"I said bad words."

"How many times?"

"About three, Father."

And so on it would go until you bled out all of your indiscretions. You knew that you could not truly be forgiven unless you told the whole story. The priest would then give you a penance of so many prayers you had to say to be absolved of these sins.

"I want you to say ten Hail Marys and five Our Fathers."

"Yes, Father."

And he would recite your absolution in Latin, "Dominus noster Jesus Christus te absolvat," as you say yours in English. Then he closes the door as he finishes, leaving you saying your piece talking to the wall. You leave the confessional and kneel somewhere else to say your penance, you know, the Hail Mary's and Our Fathers he gave you to say.

This varied from priest to priest as did the above conversation during your act of contrition. Your entire class would go at once and wait in line with the other classes. There would be more than one priest to hear the many confessions. Each priest had his own confessional. Each one had its own waiting line.

As you filed into church you jockeyed for position to make sure that you did not get the *wrong* priest. This was a calculation that seemed to elude my mathematical abilities more often than not. A few years later, Father McCredie would take his turn as Pastor of St. Mary's and he was the worst of the worst. We could hear him shouting as we each waited our turn.

"YOU WHAT!!!" and a bible slammed against something hard was all you could hear from the confessional as you waited your turn for the *execution.*

"50 Hail Marys and 20 Our Fathers!!!!" he would fire blast for all to hear.

I was always waiting for Sister Agnes to step out of the confessional in tears, but it was another fantasy of mine.

You could never hear the person confessing, not over Father McCredie. When it was your turn, you knew why. You could barely make an audible confession. Your heart would pound through your rib-cage and remove the volume right out of your speaking voice.

Whenever I had Father McCredie, I could not wait to get out and run. I stepped into the chamber of His Loudness and waited for what seemed like hours for that little door to slide, slicing into the deepest bowels of my poor sweet dear innocent life.

"Yes, my son?" as he seemed already weary from the day. This could be in my favor.

"Bless me, Father ..." I whispered.

"SPEAK UP, I can't HEAR you!!"

"BLESS me, Father, for I have sinned. My last confession was…uh…" as my voice trailed off again.

"Was WHEN!?"

"One week ago, Father."

"Hardly enough time to have any sins don't you think!?" was his form of a joke, but not a good time to laugh by any means.

"Yes, sir, but I fought with my younger brother."

"How many times?"

"Five, Father." No sense in beating around the bush.

"FIVE. In one WEEK! What else?"

I was afraid, so I lied. "Uh…Nothing, Father."

"IS THAT IT?'

"Yes, Father," wondering if that is now two lies.

"20 Hail Marys, then!" he would say as I got off too lightly.

I guess I'll have to add a few more lies to my list at next week's confession to make up for that. Usually, when I saw the other priests, I would feel so clean with the weight of my pre-teen world off of my shoulders. The air smelled so fresh. I could look up at the sky with both eyes knowing that I would surely go to heaven. After a McCredie outing, the only thing I felt was shame. I'd walk back to class with my head down for I had not confessed it all. I knew it and I knew that God knew it too. The guilt would finally pass with each telephone pole from the bus window.

"Tomorrow is Friday!"

I still received Communion the next day and I ate the bun too. Guilt decided to return. I did confess half my sins. Maybe I should have eaten only half of the bun, I rationalized. Kids will do that. What if I don't look up at the sky on the way home today? Yeah, that would do it.

Kate and the Umbrella

Roosevelt Avenue was only a block from my house. It was lined with 50-foot oak trees. There was one corner with no trees, so they put our bus stop there. They did this, so you had nothing to stand under in the rain. This could have come in handy while you waited for that big yellow taxi. The Maguire and the McBurke families were picked up the stop before me. The *boys* always saved me a seat.

Bus rides to our school must have averaged about 4 miles per hour. How else do you explain almost thirty minutes to get to a school only two miles away? I mean, I was the last stop for Pete's sake. Thirty Minutes is way too much time, a lot can happen in half an hour. Okay, maybe it was shorter than that, but I did not own a watch.

On one particularly rainy day, the door opened and I stepped onto the bus. I said good morning to the bus driver, a good man to have on your side, and then scanned for the usual group near the back of the bus. As I approached, I could see Kate, Todd's older sister, sitting in my usual seat.

Kate was two years older than us. She had Irish good looks with dark hair and a hint of freckles on her nose and high cheeks. She was very good looking, but on this day she showed a new side. Todd shrugged his shoulders, as I had to slip by Kate to sit near the window.

As the bus took off, I fell against her to give her a little reward for taking my seat and she poked me with her umbrella in the exchange. I thought it might have been by mistake, but then she did it again.

"Knock it off!" I told her. There was plenty of room between us now as she sat on the aisle side.

"Tough," she said as she poked me again.

The knock-it-off-and-tough exchange repeated several annoying times. I kept trying to deflect that metal pointed annoyance with my hands, but I was not making any ground.

"You'd better knock it off!"

"Or what?" she taunted me as she poked me again. She seemed to be enjoying this. Maybe she was thinking of becoming a nun.

Now I am totally without any defense. I started to make a fist and reared back, but *wait*… I cannot hit a girl, not even if she *is* older. I was getting angrier with each poke and I had no outlet. Finally, I found an answer. I'd spit on her. I did not say it was a good answer and certainly not one of my prouder moments, but I did, in full anger, spit at her. No, not a big juicy wet clam! I was so angry my mouth was like cotton. And so, a feeble yet meaningful spray was thrown her way.

91

She was shocked, but angry, so she poked me again. We exchanged spray and pokes only two times before she gave in.

"I'm telling," she said.

"Fine! I'll tell them about the umbrella!"

That shut her up and the rest of the trip went without incident as we stared straight ahead. When the bus arrived, she got off quickly and we both went to our respective classrooms. I was not sitting very long in class before a knock came to our door. An unattended voice from the door said that the principal, Sister Agnes, wanted Wade Morgan downstairs in her office. I took the long walk downstairs wondering what I did to warrant this. I guess I was delusional. Kate was already seated at the left side of the principal's desk with a Mona Lisa smirk. I am not sure that Kate knew what was going to follow.

Sister Mary *Guillotine* stood up and walked right towards me; I had barely reached her door.

"You SPIT on a GIRL?!!!!"

She waited for no answer as she slammed both fists into my chest knocking me backward and breathless. She proceeded to beat me, not with slaps, but with physical punches everywhere front back and finally as I ducked, she hit my hard forehead. I heard a crack. She screamed in pain, but I had no enjoyment (well maybe now as I reflect on it). Her screams of pain, gave enough pause to get a word in.

"She was stabbing me with her umbrella," I said. "I could not hit a girl, Sister."

"So you SPAT on her?!!" as she gave me the back of her other hand across my face, but she was spent. She had nothing left. So she called my house for my mother to resume the beating. My mother was there in five minutes.

They spoke inside as I sat outside the door. I did not get expelled because this was only third grade and there were five more years of beatings ahead of me.

I went home with my mom in the car and went through the usually mental "*I should have done this and I should have said that*" routine.

They were right. I should not have spat on her. I should have beaten the crap out of her, taken the umbrella, stuck it in her mouth and opened it. The mental image of that made me laugh and helped me get over it. The odd thing was that I probably would have gotten less punishment if I slammed her one. She had broken a rule that even the girls rarely crossed, she had tattled. I would never forgive her.

But I did. It did not take long before I talked to her again. After all, she did not stab me with an umbrella anymore and I don't think she knew that Agnes would beat me like that. And as I told you, she was very pretty.

Okay, fine! I'll add that to my sequel, *Confessions of a Shallow Altar Boy*.

The Conjunction

Knowing women is not rocket science; it is far more complicated than that.

4ᵗʰ Grade - Mrs. Gower

After only one year in the new school, we were sent across the parking lot to the old school. Not the one we started in, another one next to the church on Main Street. This building seemed even older than the first one. It had dark cedar shake shingles outside and equally uneven wooden floors inside.

We had the old desks again to hide our stuff and it smelled like an old nun, bat guts and sulfur. I was more experienced now, and so I felt no need to taste the disgusting desk top. The whole place smelled ready for eternal condemnation. I guess we were being punished for whatever we did last year. At least I was still with all of my friends.

I noticed that things are funnier at the most serious of times. Dull witted remarks that would typically yield a moan outside suddenly became hysterical in the classroom. The bright red faces buried under shivering shoulders were a dead giveaway. Those little side comments in church were killers, and they were always followed by a swift smack to the back of the head. Sometimes I would think of things that were so funny that I could not control myself enough to even blurt them out. So, a couple of shoulder shimmers and I'd get a smack for having *thoughts* of saying something funny.

There was another item. I am not sure where this all started, but being stupid was something we laughed at too. Dylan, Todd and I did well in school. Somehow in the midst of all our carrying on we read, we listened and we repeated back the things they told us out loud or on paper. Not so tough really. It was a lot easier than handling a bad hop at 3rd base or one of my brother's curve balls.

So naturally we made fun of dumb answers and we made fun of the kids who made them. They were stupid and they deserved it. We knew that all of the parents would be very proud of us for doing this. Well, maybe not the parents of the stupid kids. Hey, I never said that any of these were proud moments. These are true confessions after all.

"What is the largest country in Africa, Todd?"

"Egypt, Mrs. Gower."

Mrs. Gower was a bit heavy as I remember. My mom was gaining a bit of weight around that age, so I thought that this is what happens to women. They wore dresses with patterns of flowers on them. Their hair was always dark and wavy which was the style. They loved chocolate and could sit and talk about different subjects in a group without ever listening to each other.

"What is the capital of Egypt, Dylan?"

"Cairo, Mrs. Gower."

My dad was skinny and so was I. We were guys. We wore drab solid colors and we did not smell like flowers. My dad and Mr. Nelson would fish for hours without eating anything or saying a word. They packed away a bunch of beer and made a comment or two about some fish stuff. These were defining moments.

Mrs. Gower was a nice lady, but she was hard to please. She went down each row with a question for each student.

"What is the 'ship of the desert'?" she asked.

"Sahara," Kathy replied.

We all laughed, but I laughed a second past the suggested and acceptable time frame. I stood out like the guy weaving in and out of traffic and Mrs. Gower pulled me over. I had to explain this to her. "She gave the wrong answer. That was funny!"

Mrs. Gower told me that it was *not* funny. My first thought was, *"She must have been stupid in school too?"*

I flat-out did not get it. Next time I had a chance, I would make up for it, but how? I decided to be nice to a stupid kid. Mrs. Gower passed out a geography test. I could see the guy in front of me scratching the back of his head and looking out the window as if the answers were out there somewhere. This was the opportunity I was waiting for. I gave him *all* of the answers. Not only that, I casually let Mrs. Gower see how nice I was in helping him. Well, that wasn't good for her either!! She gave me a zero so I would know what really stupid felt like.

Obviously, this is a woman who cannot make up her mind. She was mean, insensitive and not as nice as I thought. Another lesson: *women are impossible to please.* I was pissed! I hate her! If you are going to act like a nun, at least dress like one! I think they make those habits in your size! I kept this little tirade to myself.

I wasn't allowed to laugh at stupid kids anymore, which took all of the fun out of fourth grade for me. I was once again reduced to snickering while the other kids were allowed to laugh out loud. I had to wait for recess to laugh.

"Hey, Todd, that was pretty funny when Kathleen said that the New Jersey was a country?"

"Yeah, Wade, we laughed when it happened, but it's over now." Todd laughed at my dilemma as he walked away.

Hey, making fun of the fact that I am not allowed to laugh isn't funny! Is it? I was glad to get out of 4th grade, get a new teacher and be able to laugh out loud once more. I would wait until Todd made a mistake and then I'll get him back for his snide comment!

I am still waiting.

Lesson 7: Coming of Age

5th Grade ~ Miss Winters

Here we go again and just when I thought that lay teachers were nuns without habits, in walks our fifth-grade teacher, Miss Winters. And what a lay-teacher she was!

It might have been *Mrs.* Winters, but we did not want her to be married. Man, she was good looking. She was tall. She was slender and she had those bumps and curves right where they looked their best. You could see her green eyes and full lips framed in thick auburn hair from across the room. She was mesmerizing.

There were days where she spoke for an hour. I would sit and stare at her as she walked back and forth. The light from the window behind her would outline her body and put a glow around that gorgeous head. As she spoke, her eyes sparkled as her dress hugged all of those beautiful gifts that God gave her. All I could hear was my heart pounding.

"Do you think that is a true statement, Wade?" she asked.

I was in sheer panic. I hadn't heard a thing. Dylan leaned over to bail me out as he whispered, "Y*es! True!*"

"Yes, Miss Winters. True!" I said with conviction as the classroom burst into laughter.

"No, no, no, it is false! Apparently, you did not understand the question," she said. Dylan could hardly control himself. Even the stupid kids were laughing.

Oh great, now she thinks I'm one of those dumb kids. This is going to suck. At least she didn't laugh at me. She'll probably do that at recess with the other teachers.

The Spelling Bee

The word 'bee' is an old term meaning a get together for a specific purpose. I would guess that all classrooms have a spelling bee, but the origin of this practice is attributed to America. The rules are simple, you miss, you lose.

Spelling is not very scientific. The rules of spelling, *like the 'i' before 'e' thing* are good standards that are meant to be broken at the most inopportune times. It really comes down to memory and language skills. Having knowledge of Latin is helpful. We used to hear the Mass in Latin, but having knowledge of Latin sounds is of no freakin' help, whatsoever.

We'd stand in a circle around the outer edges of the classroom as each, in turn, was asked to spell a word. You would say the word, spell it and then say the word again. If you missed the first word, you might as well paint a big red 'S' on your clothing. Dylan and I were pretty good spellers, but Todd was better than anyone in the school.

Our principal, Sister Agnes, was the moderator, supreme omnipotent judge, and executioner. She would come to each class personally and the winners would compete against the other classes. This meant bragging rights at some level. We did not like to lose at anything. She opened her list and went around the room again and again. About half of the class returned to their seats as she came upon Todd once again. Todd had a Clint Eastwood air about him that said, "Go ahead, nun. I can spell anything."

"Admissible," she threw out at him.

Surely a lame trick as Todd shot back, "admissible, a-d-m-i-s-s-i-b-l-e, admissible."

Dylan and I snickered as we knew Todd had bested her once again.

"That is incorrect!" She said with her own self-ingratiating smirk.

A gigantic "Huh?" echoed around the classroom.

She turned to Lana and repeated, "Admissible."

We were all shaking our heads in disbelief as Lana, now totally confused, tried to think where Todd had gone wrong. Desperately she tried a new spin on the word with an 'a.' Then Christine went with an 'e.' They were dropping like flies until Belinda repeated Todd's spelling "admissible, a-d-m-i-s-s-i-b-l-e, admissible."

"That is correct," the principal said.

"But Sister, that is exactly what Todd said" I was across the room, but I thought she was going to kill me with a fireball, that is, until the rest of the class agreed in unison.

"Yes, sister. That is what Todd said.

Miss Winters remained pretty quiet until now and then she said, "You know, Sister, I had thought that Todd had it correct, but then I thought that maybe I had heard it wrong."

"You did! Every one of you heard it wrong!" she said with her final judgment.

"Hey Sister, can you spell pompous asshole?"

She could not hear Dylan because he did not say that beyond my ears. I gave it the appropriate yet pathetic snicker as I shook my head from side to side.

"There goes our best speller," I said out loud and everyone knew it.

I gave her what she wanted. I spelled the next word wrong on purpose. I wanted no part of this anymore. I was not alone. The rift between the principal and ourselves was growing. No one ran at recess that day. We gathered in groups.

"I hate her."

"You are not alone," Dylan added.

Everyone gathered around Todd at recess, but he was speechless. Whatever influence she might have had she had totally lost us. After that, there were subtle nuances. There was a slight hesitation to stand when she came in the room.

"G'd afternoon, Sister Agnes," with a brief desk leaning stand, along with a murmur of a greeting was all she received.

Even Miss Winters referred to her as only 'the principal," and not by name. From then on we would only respect what she could do to us and the uniform. We did not respect the person inside it. Just like regular people, there were good nuns and bad nuns. If we had enough stones, we would have built a wall.

Excessively Extracurricular

Mickey Mantle[13] once said that if you added up all of his walks and all of his strikeouts, he did not touch a baseball for two years. I kind of felt this way about our 'out of classroom' experience.

We had those first Fridays, air raid drills, the stations of the cross, communion, confirmation practices, fire drills, choir practice, holy days of obligation, a religious movie in the hall, some speech about cleanliness, not to mention the odd public ridicule or verbal lynching. When I added up all of this time, I think I, like Mickey, missed two whole years of school.

These are among the consequences of going to a private school. I remember one of my public school buddies asking me a question I could not answer. I called him a heathen and wondered what the hell *science* was

---

[13] Give me a break! You need a footnote to tell you who Mickey Mantle was?

anyway. It is not surprising when we moved on to public school: they made us take remedial courses like General Science when the other kids were already taking Biology.

6th Grade - Sister Clara

For the third year in a row, we were in that old school. We were heavily in Agnes's disfavor, obviously. We dropped the Sister part and referred to her only by her name or something worse. When she visited our classroom we would give her the full greeting, but it was, as I said before, slow and almost inaudible.

Here we were in the 6th grade. We had a nun again. Her name was Sister Clara. She was taller than the other nuns. She had an almost round face and she smiled a lot. She was big-boned and pretty strong. She played baseball. She hit and threw like a guy. We figured she could kick the crap out of the other nuns. We did not tell her that because we learned our lesson with Sister Mary Lynn. We could end up cleaning a floor with a toothbrush again and Sister Clara as great as she was, was no Ingrid Bergman if you know what I mean.

"I'm going to read a few poems to you today."

"Uhhhh." you could hear the moan of every guy in the class, well almost every guy.

"Now, now, poems can be fun and after I read a few to you today, we'll have a little assignment as part of tonight's homework."

Don't you love the 'we' part? She's not writing any poem, the rest of us are!

"We will write a poem tonight, and then we'll have a little contest to see who can write the best poem."

In those days a poem had to rhyme, today's poets have lost that ability. They also did not have to recite their masterpiece in front of the entire class. First of all, I hated reading anything in front of the class. Compound this with the whisper darts from Dylan and I had no chance of getting through even the shortest verse unscathed. Whatever our poems might have been none of them were notable except Kevin's. I do remember Kevin's recital like it was yesterday. You may remember Kevin as 'The Sleepy Hollow Lake Masochist.'

Holding his paper, Kevin read proudly. "Birdie, birdie in the sky, why'd you do that in my eye."

He managed to get the final verse out before Sister Clara could close the distance on foot. Her first crack was across his knuckles. Kevin will attest to how well she hits like a guy.

"Sit down young man and give me that paper!!"

While Kevin examined his new wounds, she looked at his paper in horror. Sister Clara was pretty cool though. She did not send us to the principal like the other teachers; she gave out her own punishments. They usually had to do with writing things ten-thousand times. I had a terrible time with my attention span. Even to this day, I can handle a meeting on a subject for about 20 minutes, after that you have lost me. They have all sorts of excuses today like ADD, ADHD and ADS. In the 60s it was called a slap in the back of the head. I was sitting in class reading some assigned eye-lid dropping crap, so I kept busy filling in the white spaces on the back of my composition book.

"Wade, what are you doing?" asked the sister, as she pulled the pen from my hand.

"Uh…reading, Sister."

"Really?"

I had to write the Constitution of the United States including all of the amendments five times. She had not yet discovered carbon paper, but my sister, well experienced in such matters, filled me in.

"You can't press down hard enough to do four copies. Put two pages behind the original and the carbon in between."

I took out my fountain pen and she grabbed it almost nun-like and handed me something better.

"Here's a ball point pen. If this works, you should only have to write it twice."

"Thanks!" This was cool. It looked like I had written it and it was blue just like a pen.

"Don't mention it and, I mean, don't mention it to anyone," she said.

It looked pretty good and without the knowledge of carbon paper, Sister Clara did not suspect a thing."

"Did you learn anything by this punishment?"

"Oh yes, Sister, I learned a lot."

One day, after school, we had an intramural baseball game. I was pitching and Todd was supposed to catch, but he was late for some reason. He probably had to 'stay after' which were the words you used in Catholic school for *detention*. So Sister Clara had to put on the catcher's gear over her habit.

"Okay, Wade, let's warm up."

Let us pause a moment for that mental image.

Here I am on the mound and I stare at my new catcher in the catcher's position. She had her black habit now draped to the ground, a mask over her face and a chest-protector. It looked like I was throwing baseballs at my grandmother's black armchair. I can't throw a ball at a piece of furniture. But she pounded her catcher's mitt twice like a pro.

"Okay. Let's see what you've got."

I was laughing so hard my first couple of pitches came up 5 feet short of the plate. But she scooped them right up like Yogi and fired the ball back without getting up.

"That would be ball two. Come on Wade, you can do better than that!" She was also the umpire.

I started to fire the ball across the plate and she did not miss a beat. She snapped the ball back at me. When the first batter came up, I threw a couple over the plate. The kid wasn't too good. The order of events was pathetic. I threw the ball, the ball hit her glove and then the kid swung. "Strike two."

I was bored already, so I decided to throw a curve. It came at the batter before it's roundhouse effect took place. "Look out!" she said. The batter bailed. "Oh, sorry, strike three. You're out."

She walked out to the mound.

"Wade, I'd like you to throw the ball and let them hit it."

"Pardon me, Sister, but I am supposed to strike them out."

"Not today. We want all the kids to have a chance to hit."

"But Sister, I didn't even get to hit anyone yet."

"How's your writing hand today?'

"Okay, I'll let them hit."

I did not think that Sister Clara, who loved baseball as much as I did, would take the enjoyment out of it, not out of baseball. Only a nun would sacrifice so much.

We had a couple of innings of 'let them hit it,' but finally Todd showed up and life was back to normal. Sister Clara turned the chair covers over to Todd where the gear took on a more natural look.

"Come on Wade, no batter, no batter," Todd was merciless and I was merely following his orders.

Todd signaled for the heat and then one curve after another. There would be no snickering here and no prisoners either. Sister Clara replaced me on the mound the following inning.

Broken Wing

Ever want to take back something you said or something you did? Maybe it is just another chance, one more chance to look at it from another angle or recalculate the odds first. Maybe the word I am really looking for here is a 'do-over.'

It was another one of those afternoons under a beautiful September sky on Long Island. It was comfortable short-sleeve weather with a breath of a breeze. I went over to my friend Buddy's house like I did so many times in those years. Buddy and I grew up in the great outdoors, jumping streams, climbing trees, catching frogs, going to the beach and finding ways to live on the edge of disaster.

Buddy was almost two years younger, but his dark hair, his size, his brains and his innovation proved that we were equal. He was smart enough to be only a year behind me in school. He was advanced enough to be in some of my classes later in high school.

I was skinny. If I was a little less in the weight department, Bud made up some of that difference. He wasn't fat, he was big-boned. He looked a bit like the Beaver[14] in 'Leave it to Beaver" with only a hint of

---

[14] **Leave It to Beaver** was a 1950s and 1960s family-oriented American television situation comedy about an inquisitive but often naïve boy named Theodore "Beaver" Cleaver (portrayed by Jerry Mathers)

freckles. A tough Beaver would be more descriptive. *(Aside: Snicker)*

He did not go to St. Mary's. He wasn't even a Catholic, he was Lutheran. He was my *heathen* connection to the reality of the outside world. We were a creative team. If you took the letters of Paulsen and Morgan you could rearrange them to spell: "THIS MAY NOT GO AS PLANNED."

After we got tired of pissing on the nearest wasp nest, we would find some other activity to fill the afternoon. We'd invent games.

"Hey, let's take the swings off and swing on the top bar."

"We'll swing back and forth and jump off like they do in the Olympics."

After a few turns, "This is too boring," we thought.

We did not have uneven bars like they have in the Olympics. We only had this single cross bar. What could we do with this simple equipment?

"How about we take a running jump and catch the bar?"

The bar was a good seven plus feet off the ground and empty without the swings. From the side, it looked like two big letter 'As' joined by that high bar. That high bar was our target.

"Yeah, we'll draw a line on the ground a couple feet away and then we'll jump from there."

"Yeah, and, we'll keep moving the line back until one of us gets seriously hurt."

Actually, that last statement was not uttered. I thought that maybe one of us *should have* said that, but defeat never entered our mind. We drew a line and each of us took a few short steps in or own turn. One would jump, grab the bar, let his legs swing forward and back and then after the motion was done, we'd let go and fall gently with both feet on the ground. With each line drawn further away, the challenge got greater.

"Mark my words. This will become a new Olympic event."

"Yeah, and we will take the silver and the gold. "

I was older and had a little more jump than Buddy. I knew I could put a mark so far away from this new Olympic A-frame that he could not match it in the challenge we simply referred to as *'in a million years.'*

"Watch this!" I said. These are the two words that precede any Darwin Award[15] story.

I took a few short steps, followed by a couple of long strides and then right before the line, I leaped up, up and away. You would have thought I had a cape. "Nobody's going to match this!" were exactly my thoughts on this perfect September day. I grabbed that top bar in midair. Well, not 'grabbed' because only my fingertips got the bar. Holding as best as I could, my legs started swinging

---

[15] A **Darwin Award** is a tongue-in-cheek honor named after evolutionary theorist Charles Darwin. Awards have been given for people who "do a service to Humanity by removing themselves from the gene pool" (i.e. lose the ability to reproduce either by death or sterilization in a stupid fashion).

forward like the second hand on a clock. I would say that my legs started at four o'clock and swept right through to nine o'clock. My body was parallel to the ground and my finger hold on the bar was completely gone. I am air born.

Forget that guy on the 'agony of defeat.' I was seven plus feet in the air with no snow for a cushion. I had nothing, but air, gravity, a couple of gnats for spectators and that awful abrupt ending. That did not stop my desperate arms from grabbing for a leaf, a gnat or maybe a passing butterfly. Even those annoying mosquitoes were running from me.

Surely I must have landed on a big stick because both Buddy and I heard this loud "SNAP!" I got up from the ground almost instantaneously with the sounds of the thud and the snap. I looked back to see what stick I landed on and saw nothing, but the ground and the fact that my left arm now had two elbows.

"Oh, that's not good," I said out loud.

"Mommy!!" Buddy yelled, "Wade broke his arm!"

You see! I told you he was smart.

"Oh, Shit!" I said out loud as reality and shock took over. I did not feel a thing except fear.

I was bleeding, but believe me, that was far from the scary part. At 11, I did not know anything about medicine. I thought I might lose my arm from that brand new elbow down.

Mrs. Paulsen must have been a good athlete. She was a blur from her back door to my arm. She wrapped my arm and the rest of me in a white sheet. She was a great mom and a super lady. She made me feel that everything was going to be okay. She drove me to my house to pick up my mom. Nobody sued each other back then, so we were all able to go to the hospital together. I guess lawyers were not invented yet.

The drive was only about ten minutes. I think we made it in three. I was relieved when I found out that I was going to get to keep my arm. There was a lot of discussion between the grown-ups. There were cotton swabs, a needle or two, a few stitches and then suddenly I was exhausted. I went into this deep sleep.

I woke up that night with this beautiful white cast around my arm and it looked like I only had one elbow again. My parents took me home the next morning. Everything might have been okay, but now, after all of this, my arm started to hurt and oddly enough, I was hungry. Later in life, I would refer to this as the munchies. I could have anything I wanted to eat so we had pizza at every meal. When it was too late to get one from the store, my sister would make me some on English muffins. The sympathy thing is a good gig and you should milk at every opportunity.

I had everyone sign the cast and I wore it like a badge of honor. I ran around and played everything one-handed with that incredible cast to protect me. It was also good for what we New Yorker's referred to as s*macking someone upside the head*, not intentionally, of course. All of this running, sweating and falling on that poor cast surely reduced its useful life. Then it started to itch. It was unbearable. I used my mom's knitting needle, a ruler, a coat hanger, anything for relief. I would have poured a coke down there if I thought it would work.

Taking a shower was out. I tried it once. It destroyed my cast and had to get a new one at the doctor's office. His name was Doctor Pepper. I don't think you spelled it like that, but who cares anyway. You may remember that my other doctor's name was Doctor Candy. This drew a strange image of the medical profession. Doctor Pepper had a brand spanking new tool, an electric cast saw. He was disappointed that he couldn't use it. You could see it in his eyes as he peeled off the old cast like wet leaves off a windshield. My left arm looked so withered and the smell wasn't too swift either. It looked so defenseless in all its shriveled pathetic weakness. The doctor washed it for me. I felt like it would break while he wiped the cloth across it. I was glad when the new cast hardened. I was a bit more cautious after that. I only let people I   liked sign it. I took baths, but I did not tell anyone because, well, you know, only girls take baths.

You don't see too many altar boys with a cast, so I had a few weeks off. I guess Father McCredie felt that it wouldn't look nice to the congregation if he smacked a kid with a broken arm. He did have his good traits.

It took about 10 weeks or so for my arm to finally heal. It was a bit longer before I got my strength back in it. Buddy's dad, Mr. Paulsen, had two other younger sons.

He welded the swings back on to the swing set to prevent any further Olympic Adventures?

As for me, I still want a 'do-over'.

Italian Spice

Buddy and I would go over to the Piccolo's next door. They were pretty new to the neighborhood then. Sonny was a little younger than Buddy. He was dark haired, thin and could flip over backward without a trampoline. He had two older sisters named Joan and Janice.

"Hubba, hubba," I said to Buddy.

"What does that mean?"

"I'm not sure, but I heard the older guys say that when a girl goes by."

Joan was the oldest and she was exactly my age. Like Sonny, Joan had dark hair, but Janice was more light-headed. Okay, Janice was cute and had light brown hair. All three of them were in excellent shape. They were Italian. My father, whose character was later portrayed by Carroll O'Connor[16], called them a different name. My mother asked me not to repeat that. She did not need to tell me. I learned not to repeat most anything my father said.

---

[16] This Carol O'Connor reference is to a character he portrayed known as Archie Bunker; a veteran of World War II, reactionary, bigoted, conservative, blue-collar worker, in a TV show called All in the Family (1971-83).

The Piccolo's had a huge yard with a field on the side and these great home run hedges. It was like our own personal Wrigley field. Because of my broken arm, we'd play kick ball. After our usual impending boredom, we used a small baseball bat to hit the kickball. That was more like baseball and surely another Olympic event on the rise. We spent our time inventing more games or playing ring-a-levio.

Ring-a-levio is a simple game where everyone runs from one end of the field to the other. Everyone, that is, except the person in the middle of the field. That person tackles one of the herd as they pass by, holds them down and says "ring-a-levio, one, two, three." Now the two of them are on the same team. When the group passes again, the tackling and recruiting continues until there is only one person left. That, my friends, is the place of honor.

Tradition says that everyone must pile on the last person left.

"Nigger pile!!" someone would yell.

None of us ever gave the reference the slightest thought back then. I seriously did not connect the word nigger to a black person. It simply meant that everyone should pile on the guy at the bottom. There was a kid in St. Mary's who was black and the polite term was "colored person" in the 60's. I explained ring-a-levio to my mother one day. She explained that the term was not a nice expression, but she did not say why, so we kept using it. We teased each other about being micks, wops, kraut or a retard. To us, they were only words.

116

All I know is if you did something like a girl you were a homo, sissy or faggot. It did not mean you were a homosexual. If someone used a big word like that we would have to consult a dictionary or ask McBurke. He knew every word ever written.

More important than any stupid name was being the last person in ring-a-levio to be caught. It was the object of the game and a very proud moment, a moment that you would savor. And then you'd gasp as you could not breathe with the weight of the neighborhood upon your back. It was an honor to be piled on, so it was hard to figure that it was a bad word. It would be years before someone enlightened me.

The best part was tackling the girls and holding them a long, long time under the guise of playing the game. I would grab Joan or Janice around the waist and as gently as I could I would bring her down to the ground. Then I would hold her and I would say the slowest "ring-a-levio …one… two… three" on record. I am not sure what I liked more, tackling the girls or them tackling me. Every once in a while they would both tackle me, which is, of course, every man's dream.

When we played, Sonny almost always had the honor of being tackled last. He was pretty fast, he was tough to catch and saw no reason to let his sisters catch him. We stopped playing ring-a-levio after a few years. We listened to records more and we took walks down town or went to the movies. Joan had a friend, Leslie, who came to her house one day. She was blonde, gorgeous and was

117

developing early. I was thinking of how I would like to get my arms around her, but all that came out my mouth was, "Hey, how about a nice game of ring-a-levio?"

Go Main Street

If you are very lucky, you grow up in a small town and if this little town has a village, you are twice fortunate. Whenever we had the chance, we would take Main Street, and we still do. A good stretch of the legs in solitude was not something you opted for when you were eleven.

It was lighter this afternoon than it was the day before. Brand new leaves were taking shape on the big old maple by the church. The bright yellow flowers on the forsythia could only mean one thing.

"It is baseball season!"

It always felt warmer leaving school then going in and so it's a good day to walk home, I thought. Actually, I had no choice because the buses left an hour ago. It was the nuns' suggestion that I take the time to walk home on this most beautiful of days. It was my reward for being so well-behaved at school that day. Usually, I could count on Dylan, Kevin and the two Todds to equally behave. Once in a great while, one of us would have to make this trip all alone. It is only then that you could record your surroundings without distraction.

It is the spring of '61. I have not a worry in the world because we did not have the TV News to instill such fear.

I would go down Main Street to Grant Avenue, a direction the boys would argue against, using logic like, "What are you, freakin' stupid?" It was a bit longer, but there's more to see.

With no one there to insult me, I headed directly across the street and planned to head due west. A guy named Mr. Ripken owned a luncheonette for a short time in East Littleton right across from the church. His daughter Tricia was my cousin's girlfriend.

I reminded him that we were sort of related.

"Hi, Mr. Ripken, I'm Jamie's cousin, Wade."

"How are you?"

"Just fine. Can I have a coke, please?" I guess he liked Jamie so much that he only charged me full price.

Oh, well, it is baseball season and I can barely contain myself. My bag of books in one hand and juggling a soda in the pocket of my baseball glove in the other; I headed the two miles toward my house, *my way*.

There are two Victorian houses on the north side of the street. If you had one, you had to paint it white in those days because it was the law or something. The East Littleton Movie Theatre was across on my left. The marquis said, NOW PLAYING – *Inherit the Wind*. This was a total lie because it was 4:00 on a weekday afternoon.

Map of Main Street, Littleton

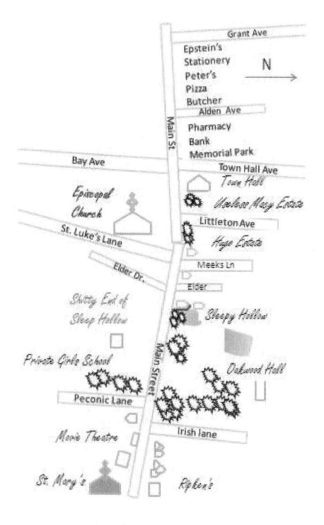

Now playing, my ass! Nothing *is* playing 'right now' and thank God for that, a car mechanic was next to the theater. He made so much noise as he worked, no one would be able to hear the film.

A slicked-back, dark-haired, oil-smudged guy in once clean Quaker State overalls, popped his head out from a car as if he read my mind. I was going to mention something about the noise, but I waved and he waved back. Chalk this up to *respect* which is something we all had for adults back then.

I kept drinking while balancing my stuff and finally reached Irish Lane, which seemed to take forever. I would not feel that lengthy road sensation again until the late 60's, but it would be accompanied by a good case of the 'munchies' and a stop at the Carvel Ice Cream store.

As I looked down the lane, I could see one of our *alleged* shorter routes north. Shaking my head, I kept going, my way, west.

"Not today guys! Today I am going this-a-way," I said as I crossed the lane.

Just before a big field, there were woods on my right with those nasty vines and sticker bushes that sneakily try to hide behind more yellow flowers. God, I hate those things. If you lost a ball or yourself in these woods, you always had to go through these thorny plants that seemed to appear from nowhere. Once you were in them, they would grow around and behind you. You would have to scratch your way out of them. You would emerge looking like the loser in a cat-tossing contest. Even worse, you could end up being one of those missing children. Being missing back then would suck because milk still came in glass bottles so there would be no place to post your picture.

Well, no use dwelling on this; I had nothing in those bushes that I needed.

"Oh wait! There's a hard ball in there!"

Ten minutes later, completely poked and scratched beyond any repair, me and my brand new useless water-logged Official Imitation American League baseball, headed toward Littleton. I had these stupid daydreams, for example, if there were a car coming in the opposite direction, I would use a pole to block me from sight. You had to walk at the right pace and speed up at the end. If you did not do it right, the car would see you, and you would invent some consequence for your failure like angry dogs will attack you at the next corner. Avoiding cracks on the sidewalks was another favorite superstition.

I would walk three telephone poles and then run five. It is hard to run with a bookbag without looking faggy, so I gave that idea up after my second attempt to look cool.

There was a stretch of land, a field actually, that was called Oakwood Hall. I never associated or saw any building on this land and thought it odd to call it a *hall*. There really was an orphanage deep on the other side of the woods, which accounted for the name, but I never saw it. I shrugged my shoulders and figured there was some grown up with a naming convention issue. As if there weren't enough confusion another group simply referred to the whole area as Sleepy Hollow Lake.

Oakwood Hall and its field bordered on that lake which froze over for ice-skating, but not now, it is spring time. Summer would soon be here and you know what that means? I would not be passing this way again until next September. There's no point in stopping if Kevin isn't with me as you well know. I kept walking down Main and I saw a street called Elder Drive with some houses along the lake. I never noticed the houses. That must have been nice to live there. We used to play in the streams and that lake. I wondered if they enjoyed the view along with our blood-curdling screams and obscenities.

A few more telephone poles and I passed Dr. Glinick's house as I see the sign for Meeks Lane. Meeks Lane?

"I guess these are people who will inherit the earth," I said, with a snickering smile. I am hoping that God appreciates my sense of humor more than the nuns do.

There is another doctor's house across from Dr. Glinick's. This guy scared me because people would go in, but no one would ever come out. It might be because I always went by at 4:15, but timing and impressions are everything. I blamed my reputation at school on such things.

A few newer houses are springing up behind the doctors' houses, but there is nothing after them but this big sprawling mansion. Some people in my town had some serious money. We did not have any money... seriously.

My brother said, "My friend, Peter Ivan, lives in this house." It was bigger than my school. I never met him so, in my mind, I was not sure that he really existed.

"Hey! I am still trying to get the whole I can't see God, but he exists concept down so don't be throwing Peter Hugo at me."

Some shrink would probably claim some psychological damage from Richie's "Mr. Hand" puppet days.

The Ivans had another little house close to the gate. It was bigger than what I lived in. I'd hate to mow that lawn! We only had one of those things you pushed around.

I figured a game of hide-and-go-seek in the mansion would take about…hmmm… about two…. maybe two and a half days in there. My friend Jerry could probably give you a better estimate. You would have to give him the exact number of rooms, closets and the size of the furniture. I hadn't quite met Jerry yet. If I had I would have had to ask the Ivans for a tape measure and a few hours to gather some facts.

Across the street is the beautiful St. Luke's Episcopal Church. This is where the nuns told us that *heathens* went to worship their God. Later it would become a form of personal worship known as the Boy Scouts where I could ask Jerry more of my serious math questions and play dodgeball. It's a good commercial break from our walk down Main to talk about the wonderful experience known as 'The Boy Scouts of America.'

Boy Scouts

We were thirteen when we entered the Boy Scouts and we met on some scheduled day of the week at St. Luke's Church in their... *oughta...*, this big freakin' room with a stage. A significant part of our fun and laughter came from playing dodge-ball. We did not play dodge-ball at St. Mary's which is a shame. I could see the blur of a black habit parallel to the ground, diving behind a tree to avoid one of our *errant* throws.

My interpretation here may be all wrong, but the public school kids came here for some much-needed discipline, and we were there to let loose. We would have this pretty serious meeting with Mr. B, whose real name was Baddick. He was our Scoutmaster. The irony here was that he was a   great guy with a terrible name. We could have had fun with that name, but we did not make fun of nice adults. Oh well, maybe our next mean principal would be Sister Mary Killpecker and we could make use of our material.

After Mr. B's meeting, we would split off into individual patrol meetings where we would go off into separate rooms. There were six in our room and Jerry Newport was our Senior Patrol Leader. Jerry was cool. He was two years ahead of us in school and light-years ahead of us in everything else. His hair was nearly white like mine and of course, he was taller. He had badges on his badges and knew every page of the book we needed to learn. But this book was a lot more fun than anything I had read until I got one with a centerfold.

Jerry taught us how to do stuff like tie knots and then he would leave, probably out of frustration. He would go off to see the other Patrol Leaders for their meeting. He would close the door behind him and that's when the squirrel fights began.

I had no idea what that meant either. About 15 seconds after Jerry left, the lights went out, and I heard, *"Squirrel fight!"* and suddenly someone attached a pair of pliers to my nuts and was not letting go. We had this guy in our patrol who was handicapped but not in his grip. I had to beg for mercy before he'd let go.

Jerry probably wondered why I sat in the corner with my book and then faced the wall each week before he left. He probably thought it was a Catholic thing.

Maybe we can get back to the scouts later, but I need to finish that walk home.

Remember the Main

It was difficult to take in the panorama of St. Marks Church and the Hugo estate all at once. If you were not careful, you might cross Littleton Avenue without looking as you kept staring back. But today I would not be hit by a car. I would save that for another day.

Littleton Avenue was another acceptable route home for the boys, but only if we were stopping at Sleepy Hollow Lake. After you had passed Littleton Avenue, I was in 'what-are-you-stupid' territory. Nobody went this way. It did take longer, but as we got older, Main Street was definitely the way to go.

There was some nondescript land to the right which was supposed to have belonged to a guy a named Macy. We thought it was the real Macy, but it was another guy who did not run the parade or anything worthwhile. We called this the 'Useless Macy estate.

There were maples, oaks and sappy pines, more nasty bushes without baseballs. A short-cut bicycle path toward the bowling alley was there. Bowling was invented for kids who sucked at baseball. Bowlers have a strange way about them, almost a cult. A bowling ball has four holes, three in the ball and the hole holding it. Even if you could not play any sport at all, you could still bowl. A lot of the hoods liked it because you could smoke while you bowled. You can't ride a bike with a bowling ball and look cool, not even if you had a Lucky Strike hanging from your lips. It can't be done.

Later in life when we all take up bowling we would wish we had started it sooner.

Nobody that I hung with took this path or bowled back then. My friend, Jackie was the exception. I saw him roll two 300 hundred games at different times. He had more and he was the best bowler Littleton ever saw. I believe he won a few state championships, AND he was a good baseball player.

Just like in life, some rules were meant to be broken. A guy like Jackie passes this way only once and he left us way too early. God bless you, Jackie.

Town Hall

After the path, there was this stretch of nothing until you get to the Big *Nothing* called **Town Hall.**

It was on the right at the circle, and I had no idea what on earth this place was or what they tried to accomplish in there. Nearly fifty years later I am even less educated.

With the same old tired blood year after year, my mother would say, "They are steeped in complacency." Then I would go ask Todd what that meant.

I found that it was not what they tried to accomplish, it was more about what they worked so hard to *prevent.* The only positive functioning force seemed to be the Planning Department.

Today, I am proud to say that the town   does look beautiful and I say this for three reasons:

1. Todd works in there.
2. Todd can always be counted on to do the right thing and
3. He's still bigger than I am.

The town hall was smaller back in '61 without any wings to the east or west. After many years of raising the taxes for no reason, they built extensions. It was not big enough to contain all of their tax increase-progress prevention measures.

The residents south across Main share that same street, but declare their side to be called *Bay Avenue*. I took this as a form of protest to separate them from the *enemy*.

In ironic contrast, the Memorial Park lies next to the "Tax" Hall. I thank the Lord it is still there today. Here stands our finest moment as a tribute to all of those who have served our country and gave their lives for us. It is beautiful and you cannot pass it by without emotion. God bless them.

Bank On It

The First National Bank on the right was a pretty big building in its day. It was kind of a tan-yellow pillared strong-looking shoe-box structure and made you feel safe to put your money in it.

Back in '61, I had a Christmas club in that bank that I put fifty cents in each week for fifty weeks. Well, actually my mom put it in each week. In the end, they would give you $25, so you could buy presents. By my calculations that meant they did not give up any interest. Bastards! *(Oops, add one to my bad word count.)*

I had suggested that the next year my sister and brothers would agree to keep the 50 cents each week. What a nice Christmas present that would be for each for us. Not a present once a year but every single week. Imagine an extra 50 cents each week! I pitched this logic to Mom. She called me humbug which basically meant that it was not to going to happen, not on Maddox Street.

After not paying interest on my Christmas club for a few years the bank was able to buy the lot across the street and add an extension.

There was a pharmacy near the bank. In 1962, it was a Rex-All drug store and my mother used to recall this earlier story about my sister.

Julie wondered off in the drug store when she was about 4 years old and went up to the counter with a candy bar.

"Can I have this?" she asked about as cute as four can be.

"It's 5 cents. Do you have any money?" he replied about as cute as forty could reply.

Julie said no and left the candy bar on the counter and walked away. Seemingly the transaction was over. Julie pondered her dilemma. Figuring the odds of getting 5 cents from my mom, she decided to go next door to the bank.

All that the lady teller could hear was this little voice obviously attempting to rob the bank.

"Can I have money please?"

The lady leaned over the top of the counter and saw this little girl with blue eyes.

"Do you have money here? The man at the store said I need 5 cents."

Somewhere in the laughter that surrounded the bank floor, 5 cents made its way to the palm of my sister's hand. She said, thank you and walked out without the least bit of surprise on what had happened.

She picked out another candy bar and brought it to the counter and with a confident face handed the man 5 cents.

"Thank you," he said.

"Thanks," said Julie as she ripped the candy from its paper holster and took her first bite.

"Where did you get that?"

My mom would not find out until she went to make her most embarrassing deposit next door.

Paper Routes

Since Mr. Ripken' Luncheonette ripped me off by charging me for the soda, I did not have enough money left to buy anything. I admit that I did take a brief look at the bank. It was closed. Thank God. The last thing we needed was another embarrassing story. I smiled and kept walking.

Soon I would have my paper route and all of these lovely stores would be at my mercy. The town became my paper route, the worst route any carrier could have.

The pharmacy would barter a paper for a Reese's Peanut Butter Cup every day and I'd have to make up the difference at the end of the week.

The bank and the pharmacy were the beginning of my route. As long as we are going this way, I'll take you on the 5 cent tour and more the life in the 1960's. After swapping the paper for a Reese's at the Rex-All pharmacy, I headed west on the north side of main. The first place was the site of the town hall many, many years before my time. It was so many things even in those days I could not keep track. I delivered to a businessman who rented the office. He did not sell anything to eat, drink or throw so he paid me for the paper to subsidize my habit.

I walked across Alden Avenue which seemed to hide among the busier streets. I had to drop papers at the corner store and the butcher. I would have swapped for some bologna, but the smell of the bakery was drifting over my head. With a long concentrated inhale I could capture and identify every confection.

"Jelly donut, please?"

"That'll be 5 cents."

Funny, that is the exact price of the paper.

"Trade?"

"Sure."

The Indians traded trinkets for land, but I got jelly donuts for a mere Newsday. I was king! I was not even 5 feet tall and weighed less than 75 pounds, which made people wonder.

"Where does he put it all?"

Littleton took forever to get its own Pizza place and it was my downfall. The space was so narrow it was hard to believe there was room for a store. Getting two regular-sized people in there was impossble.

I saw this big guy who looked like he had already eaten a few pies, so I had to ask, "Are you in line, sir?"

"Go ahead. I'm waiting for my pie."

Now that I reflect on it, that guy was always on his way in or out of that store.

At 15 cents a slice, it was three times the cost of a candy bar or a cheese bun, and he would not take three papers, so I had to pay for this.

"That'll be 1.25," Sal said to the big guy.

"Wait a minute," and I thought, eight slices at 15 cents a slice, that's only $1.20. So I ordered 8 slices.

"Do you want a whole pie?" asked three-fingered Louie.

His name wasn't Louie, but *Three-fingers-Sal* doesn't jive.

"No, thank you, just eight slices, please."

What dummies, I thought. Now I got a whole pie for $1.20 and saved 5 cents for a coke. Jerry would be so proud of me. "Here you go," Sal said as he gave me eight slices on waxed paper.

"What about a box?' I asked.

"Sure, that will be 10 cents," Sal said. Okay, so maybe Jerry doesn't need to hear about this transaction.

I usually shared my pizza with anyone who helped me with the route that day. Eating four slices was not a problem, but I lost 5 cents on the deal and eating them without a drink was a dry awakening.

Next to the pizza place was a bunch of useless places I could not trade with places like the insurance guy and a hairdresser. Finally, you were rewarded by the sweet smells of Peter's Candy Kitchen. My friend's dad owned the place. I was not about to get anything for the price of a paper. They did make their own over-priced candy. It was the good stuff. It was well over my head and means. My mom bought our Easter candy there and she managed to get most of it, intact, back to the house.

Peter's was a landmark. They had a jukebox, milk shakes, burgers and the best ice cream and sodas in town. They had red leather booths and red leather stools at the counter. The floors were big white and black squares that matched the bobby sox and saddles shoes that walked upon them. Everything smelled delicious. I felt out of place delivering the paper with all of those older kids around who never gave me a second look, except maybe my sister. "What are you doing?"

"Delivering the papers, for the tenth time this week!" I exaggerated.

I think she wanted to make sure that the other kids knew that I wasn't sent there to check up on her. My sister did not wear bobby sox or poodle skirts. If she were in *Grease*, Olivia Newton John would not have played her part. She was one of those girls that went out with those tough guys. I'll save Peter's for another day. I already had four slices and I think I am going to ralph a few up.

The Worth's Stationery Store was next, and he did not get a paper. Actually, he sold papers and I was competition. I only stopped by once.

"Would you like the paper delivered?'

Mr. Worth stared through me. Mafia consiglieres would come for miles to study this look. My blood turned

134

cold as if I had seen a nun in my bedroom. I held the paper like a protective vest and walked out backward to my next delivery.

"Any news sales this week?" the manager would recite.

"Yeah, Mr. Worth at Worth's Stationery wants 30 papers a day, but he wants you to see him personally."

"Yeah, right," he said.

After the exchange, I made my way down the street. I delivered to the apartments above the stores and thought how neat it would be to live there. I lived a mile from these stores and we only had a deli close by. I stopped at the town Deli and then Epstein's. They were like the five-and-dime but then, not really. Epstein sold more clothes. They had very few toys and no army men in the package like the guys across the street. They had no baseball stuff at all except a jock strap.

"This place is worthless," I thought as I dropped off the paper.

After a few hundred jelly donuts, pizza, Almond Joys and Reese's they took that paper route away from me. My parents had to take out a loan to cover my sugar habit and the rehab that followed. I got a new route closer to home and much too close to a pair of German shepherds.

Heading Home

Well, my route went further down Main Street, but on my walk home from school that day, this was a right turn. Since there were no more places to trade we might as well head back to my house. I made the right on Grant Avenue and headed north. A few blocks on the right was the home of my friend Bobby Sienna. Bobby went to St. Mary's House of Torture with us, but smartly opted for public school before the sixth grade. This was a major coup. My sister had made the same jump and damaged any chances of my escape.

"Your brother Richie graduated *with honors*," my mother would say.

I would graduate with the honors called 'ruler tattoos.'

We would not catch back up with Sienna until high school where he had a couple of years' head start on the real meaning of life.

No time to stop at his house, it's getting late and the beer and soda place is closing. My older brother worked there some times and if I timed it right, I could get a free coke. Up Grant Avenue, across Union and over the tracks was half of the trip home from town. I got there too late.

"Morgan? Oh, yeah he left about 2 minutes ago."

I could see him in the distance as I made my left on Moffitt Blvd. He lifted weights and his arms stuck out of his straining t-shirt when he walked. There was no mistaking that fast gate. I ran to catch him, but I barely caught him by the time we got to the house. If I had seen a film of me running with this book-bag in one hand and my glove in the other, I'd have to beat myself up. I think I mentioned that there is no manly way to run with a book-bag.

"Want to have a catch?"

"Sure."

It did not matter who asked and who accepted in this exchange. It was an exchange we had delivered hundreds of times before. Our five years difference did not matter, we had one thing in common, baseball. Richie would tell me of the great ball players. He did not like the Yankees, but he admired them.

"They can beat any other team with their bench players."

He was a Milwaukee Braves fan and he followed Eddie Matthews like I worshipped 'the Mick.'

He would teach me not to be afraid of the ball, which was something that I would keep hidden and would face on every ground ball.

"Be a man. Don't turn your head!"

Ironically we played the position of each other's hero. Richie played center field and I, like his hero Eddie Matthews, played third base. A third baseman is like a hockey goalie except that he has no padding, no mask and no brains. Hundreds of thousands of ground balls, one-hoppers, bad bounces and 32 stitches, I had a healthy respect for that horsehide. I was more afraid of missing the ball than getting hit. Letting the team down is far more painful.

Lesson 8: Altar Egos

The Church Itself

If you are looking for stories of abused altar boys and deviate priests, you are going to have to find another book. My personal feeling is that if you put a hundred people in a room of any profession, a few perverted characters will surface. We had no such experiences, so I will not invent any here. This is about a bunch of guys with a necessary service to perform with an incredible sense of dignity and humor.

St. Mary's in the 60s made you take notice. For sure it was the pure white structure that caught your eye as you drove by. Walking speed was better and gave the church its proper inspection. The beautiful statue of Mary and the flower gardens gave you a reason to stop. It still stands as proud as a grand oak on Main Street in East Littleton to help us remember our own roots.

The outside was darkly weathered cedar-shake and then renovated to white clapboard at that time. It gave it a grand and clean look, but today they have reverted back. It does not catch the eye the same. It is difficult to see why, maybe like the Town Hall, they became complacent and the maintenance is easier. Or maybe it is too much change for my selfish memories.

If you ever go back to any place it always looks so much smaller than you remembered. The first time I walked in I was at the other end of my mom's hand. I could not believe the dizzying ceiling. It was so high there were clouds. I wasn't sure, but they were part of the painting on a perfect blue sky with angels.

"So this is heaven," I thought.

The altar was a hundred feet away, and it was made of gold from the floor to what would have been the top of my house. Some of it was paint, but there was a lot of real gold too. The ornate structures of the altar, the columns, the artwork and the statues, held your eyes and made you wonder. It put you in a state of awe. This was the experience and part of its purpose, but that would all change in time.

Father Henry

You would think that Saturday would have been a day of some reprieve. After all, we had school all week and church on Sunday. Certainly, Saturdays would be held …well, let's not say *sacred*, because I don't want to rot in hell like they predicted. But Saturday mornings we gave up for our meetings. You had to to be an altar boy. There you would get your mass assignments for the week along with some comments from the priest in charge.

But it was okay, mostly because we had this young priest that ran the meeting. His name was Father Henry and he was from Brooklyn. Even if a sentence was not really a question, he would add the word "Eh?" I guess it was like our annoying "you know?" that we added as a hesitation to see if anyone is paying attention.

"So, you want to be an altar boy, eh?"

Not the Fonzie "Ehhh," but the Brooklyn one. It was closer to the Canadian "Eh," but with a Brooklyn attitude.

Father Henry was younger than most priests that we knew. I guess that would be true even if he were 50, but he was barely 30. He was a bit taller than the others. He looked to be in good shape with his dark brown hair and brown eyes. He had this permanent smirk on his face that could only come from years of Catholic schooling and getting away with stuff.

He had an air of confidence, but there was not a pompous bone in his body. He had a great smile and he made us laugh. He was a real person. He was cool. He taught us Latin. Well, he taught us to make Latin-like sounds is probably more accurate.

We would rattle off something that sounded like "gobby, gobby, howie, zowie, zowie." Now, we were cool, too. We were altar boys. We were allowed places where the rest of the congregation was not. Like on the Altar or where they kept the wine.

There are various types of church services an altar boy gets to perform. Some are very desirable, some are not.

141

Early masses suck; weddings and funerals are the best because you got tips. You had to know when to kneel, sit, stay and speak and what to do and where to walk. It was like being on stage, but we tried not to think of that. That might make you nervous.

Unlike a test in school, there seems to be no intelligence requirement for being an altar boy. I mean it's not like the girl's beauty school where you could actually flunk out. I have to say most of us did know our stuff. It is just that sometimes we'd forget. After a good number of weeks of forgetting, Father Henry, nice as he was, seemed a bit *pissed* (and not in the Irish way).

"You guys... You fool around... You want to play with the girls! You come to church, you don't know your Latin!?"

We knew he was mad because he did not add the necessary 'eh?' to any of his sentences.

"I ask for volunteers for the 6:30 Mass… no hands!! I ask for volunteers for a wedding, all the hands go up.!! You say a couple of howie, zowie, zowies…and…Where's my 5 bucks?!!!" as he gestured an open hand. He was right, and we knew it.

We all felt so bad that we all volunteered for 6:30 Mass. We still volunteered for the weddings and the funerals. We were sorry, not pitiful. Besides we knew this wasn't coming from Father Henry. It was actually coming from our *beloved* pastor, Father McCredie.

Father McCredie's Life Lessons

If you love someone, you find ways to respect them. You overlook their faults and forgive an indiscretion or two. But fear breeds hatred and contempt and not respect, hatred does not forgive easily.

We only feared the man we simply referred to as McCredie. He was our Pastor. He was a bulky man but not fat. His thick hands and forearms gave him a look of strength. He had rugged features, but his skin was a bit whiter than it should have been which gave him that added scary appeal. The only exception was his nose, which was often red as were the tips of his ears. He looked like he was about to explode and too often he did not let you down. If he smiled, we never saw it. If he laughed, we never heard it. He was true fire and brimstone and his sermons were about the dark side of man and his inevitable burning in hell.

It was preordained that in the rotation you would have to serve one of his masses. By the time McCredie came into town, we were seasoned, veteran altar boys with a full year and more than 50 services under our belt. We knew our *merde*, but not well enough for him.

During the ceremony of the Mass, the two altar boys would each bring up a crucible, one filled with wine, the other with water. The priest would hold out the chalice, and each boy would pour a quantity of each. The amount of water and the amount of wine depended on the priest. You knew how much to pour. The priest gave you that

143

inaudible look a Jewish husband gives his wife when the table salt was missing.

For McCredie, the water might as well have been empty. I once and only once made the mistake of pouring the water before he could present his glare. This was our first meeting. Since this was only half way through the ceremony, I was both stirred and shaken. I walked like a Geisha on rice paper through the rest of the mass.

So much has changed in the mass. I am not going to reflect on whether it is for the better. It has changed. Altar boys and the mass itself have buried the Latin. That's easier on the boys, but then again, you can't fake knowing the words with a couple of gobby-gobbies, either.

The priest used to face away from you as he prepared the sacrament. The sacrament is the host, you know, the host …the little wafers? Yeah, now you've got it. Anyway, this provided a few moments of relief with his back to us. Now, facing the congregation, he sees the altar boys the entire time. That can't be good. I can't imagine serving an entire service with McCredie looking at me.

He wasn't very pleasant to the congregation either. After all, it's not like he had to be elected or anything. His sermons, as I said, were about sin. What a surprise. Even Communion (serving those little wafers) was a trauma. I was surprised that anyone felt worthy to receive. He would place the host on each one's tongue with his large dry fingers as the altar boy would hold a gold plate beneath their chin. You were supposed to catch the host if someone were to drop it. This is where I learned that you are not allowed to slip and say, "Oh, shit!" especially in church. I deserved that slap for sure.

In the back of the church, behind the altar, we drank his wine and replaced it with equal parts of water. Vengeance was not ours to give, but this action was not without cause. This next episode must be written to understand our call for deliverance.

As the economy fluctuated, our parents had their ups and downs. There would be lay-offs from businesses, a divorce and maybe even a death in the family. People would still buy food for their family, gas for their cars, fuel for their homes and pay their mortgage, if too little were left over, the school tuition would be late. McCredie, as our Pastor, was also in charge of the school. He was as tolerant of such things as he was in everything else in his kingdom. And so he would summon the children whose parents had not paid, right in front of their classmates to ridicule them.

"YOUR parents have not paid YOUR tuition. This school is not a CHARITY, and we EXPECT payment this week for ALL of YOUR outstanding tuition. DO I MAKE myself CLEAR?" and he would tell each child how late each one was with the same compassion and the same audience present.

The children would crawl back to their seats trying to find some way to hide their shame and their tears.

So Father McCredie, I surely hope I do not rot in hell like you said that I would. I know that God is just and,

145

perhaps if He is forgiving, you and I will not have to sit next to each other for all eternity.

Peace be with you and may God have mercy upon us.

Father O'Sullivan

A few years later they replaced Father McCredie with Father O'Sullivan. It might have been delusional, but we wanted to think we had something to do with this. Father O'Sullivan was more like Father Henry. He never ever yelled at us on the altar or anywhere. He never embarrassed us and he did not care how much wine or water you poured. I am sure he would not like us drinking it, so I stopped. I did not like it anyway.

The new pastor would stop by your classroom about once a month it seemed. Father O'Sullivan was a welcome sight next to his evil predecessor. He would come in with Sister Agnes and the entire class would rise with the same old sing-song greeting.

"Good af…ter…**noon**…Fath…er. Good after…**noon**…Sister," and then we would sit down.

The pastor would tell us something nondescript and Sister Agnes would nod her head up and down. She looked like a Bobblehead doll; kind of like the vice president looks when the president speaks at the State of the Union, you know, pathetic. I took a sick enjoyment from those moments because it made our dear principal subservient and quiet for a blessed moment.

Father O'Sullivan never seemed to have anything unpleasant to say in contrast to our principal. They would continue to play good-cop, bad-cop though the rest of our parochial lives. His sermons were born from goodness, about heaven and how to get there. His stories after the gospel of the mass captured our imagination, our attention and our devotion.

"Good morning," he would say cheerfully. "Today I want to talk about heaven, a road which we are all bound for…"

You would leave mass feeling good about yourself for having been there. And that is the way church should always be, not leaving with empty hearts and pockets with fear and sadness.

"God bless you, Father O'Sullivan. We do not have to ask where you are."

Partners

Your partner on the altar was chosen by height and nothing else. I was one of the shortest in the class. I was a tough little kid as altar boys go. My partner was a kind and gentle soul, a soft marshmallow with black hair but a rock-solid altar boy for sure.

My other buddies were taller, so they got partners that were closer in demeanor. They were also closer to their interests. They could share a few sips of wine in the back, I had to sneak mine. And so, I was shamed into the act of *drinking alone,* thereby becoming an alcoholic all because of Alfred.

Alfred was pious. He held his hands in prayer high under his chin. He tilted his head like an angel, like my dog Daisy did when she did not understand something. I was certain he would be a priest someday. I wanted to give him early sainthood a few times myself. Every Saturday morning he would volunteer for the 6:30 Mass.

"Hey! I'm your partner, remember? How about a nice wedding?"

My brother Richie was an altar boy before me. I think that he was better at this than I would ever be. I know that Alfred was. He knew every word of Latin, pronounced it perfectly; he knew where to stand, kneel and when to *go deep.* He knew the playbook by heart. I used him to reassure what it is we were supposed to do as I was easily distracted.

My mom and Alfred's family sat near the front. These were proud moments for her. I wished she would come to my ball games as devoutly, but you don't get to choose your moments and neither did she.

Our parish outgrew the size of our church, so we had to expand services into a little hall next door to the Rectory. Things on that altar were much closer. The entire stage was only 10 feet deep at best. Add the makeshift altar and that only left about 7 feet of depth for the priest and the 2 altar boys.

It stood about 3 feet higher than the main floor with no railing. This made it seem even tighter, especially with an over-expressive priest on board.

Father Garcia, whose dramatic, over-accentuated movements should have been put to music, was from South America. He was as small as Alfred and me, but his Spanish exaggerations and exacting annunciation were only exceeded by his tremendous wingspan. He had unusually long arms for his size.

On this day, *I can almost hear Ed Sullivan*," right here on our stage..." Father Garcia bows over the altar, straightens up, takes a step backward and proclaims in Latin, "O-RAY-moos!" as he spreads his enormous wings. I see it coming. I ducked. Alfred did not. The sound of a *SMACK* sent poor Alfred and his perfectly held hands flying off the stage.

"He made Alfred disappear!" I thought.

I turned around and looked behind me and then I looked three feet down. It didn't even look like Alfred. His vestments pulled high over his head were a mere pile on the floor. It looked more like the bottom of my brother's closet. I heard Alfred moan. He was okay.

The crowd was appalled at first by the crumbled remains of Saint Alfred, but then they noticed something else. The other altar boy was doubled-over in laughter. It looked like a scene right out of the Three Stooges and, in this otherwise solemn moment, I could not help myself.

"Isn't that Mary Morgan's boy?"

"Wait till she hears about this!"

"She's right there you idiots," I thought.

They all gathered up Alfred and his shoes. It took quite a while for us to get back to the mass. Father Garcia was pretty shaken up himself. Alfred was okay, but his parents insisted on taking him home. People were always finding reasons to bug out early. Then there was the excruciating murmuring about my indiscretion.

"Hey! This is church! Shut up already!"

I only thought that, but they must have read that in my look because they finally did. Father apologized to the congregation and assured them that his young holiness was just fine.

I had to finish the mass alone with Father Spread Eagle. His gestures were much more subdued and he kept looking back to see if I was still there. Somehow I was going to be punished today and then again tomorrow at school. Hey! I did not cause this to happen.

Alfred's mom wouldn't let us be partners after that. Father O'Sullivan and Father Henry didn't yell at me at all. They figured that the possessed screams of Sister Agnes were more than enough. Oh well. No more volunteering for 6:30 Mass and a new partner whom I might share a few sips with.

I got a new partner who knew less than I did. Alfred, where are you? I miss you.

7th Grade ~ Sister Thomas

Sister Thomas was possibly the most notorious nun of all time. Her reputation was like a tsunami of fear that preceded her. We would cautiously whisper after she walked by (a couple hundred yards or so). My brother had her when he was in 7th grade. He would tell me stories about her strict punishments and a 4-foot ruler that she wielded like the Sheriff of Nottingham. She even looked like a smaller wrinkled version of Basil Rathbone in a habit.

Maybe I could quit before the 7th grade like my friend Bobby Sienna did. He and his wrists went on to public school and lived happily ever after. Our parents were friends and Bobby would tell me about public school. They went on lots of field trips, they didn't have any tests and they had a gym they played sports in all day long. We had a dirt parking lot to play on and one trip a year chaperoned by nuns.

In those days St. Mary's had 30 angels in each class. Picture, if you will, 60 seventh-graders, only half of which would have to have Sister "Tommy-gun" while the others were in full gloating celebration. Based on the alternating formula of the classes the other class should have gotten Thomas. But it was easy for Agnes to pull the strings and make sure that her *favorite* class would end up with her favorite Hench-nun.

Her wiry bones draped her habit as if it were still on the hanger. Her reputation seemed out of place. She was frail, I had expected bigger. She had wrinkles, I had expected warts. I   expected shoes that curled upwards and a pointed hat. Her habit was crisp and neatly ironed in contrast to her face. She was older than her years, but she *was* consistent. If she had a good mood, it never showed itself. She had the tiniest little mouth and her face was drier than the parking lot. With her back still toward you, she could spin her head around and her eyes could burn a hole through you. She was whiter than anyone I had ever seen that was still alive. I was more afraid of her than Father McCredie, himself. And here we are at the very height of our impish years.

She was many things, but she was very holy. This should work for us. We were, after all, not just students, we were *Altar Boys*. It was not to be. She was fair in that she treated everyone with equal disdain.

"I remember your brother Richie and your sister Julie. Which one are you like?" she asked in her *special, kind* way.

"Richie, Sister," I guessed.

"Oh? I suppose you think your way to heaven is through baseball

There was a hint of a small smile on her face. This scared the crap out of me. Surely a smile would cause her face to split open and some little kid that she had eaten would spill out on the floor.

There was no way I was going to win. I can't imagine what would happen if I said, Julie. Julie's stories of

Tommy-gun were even scarier than Richie's. I think I'll just shut up and answer.

"No, Sister." I'd rather wimp out and get beat up in the play yard than face her again.

Saving Face

Thomas was the toughest teacher you would ever meet. To get away with something was temporary, but if you truly, truly got away with it, you were a star. You would be idolized, privately and nervously idolized.

She had secret cameras before there were cameras. She sucked the blood from her victims long before the vampires that copied her black cape. Her wrinkles were not wrinkles, they were notches of her many kills. If you dared to cross her, you were king for a day or maybe king for one brief moment. And such a moment belonged to me on this one beautiful, perfect spring day.

Once in all history, one may return to a parochial classroom from lunch before a teacher, but never a nun, that is until this fine day. Today, Sister *somebody-please-iron-my-face* was late. She was very late. I'd say at least two minutes. All of these great thoughts went through my head. Maybe she poked Kate McBurke with an umbrella. Maybe she went across the street for a cup of coffee. And maybe Sister Disgusting was going to whip her in front of the entire school for being "tardy"! A sadistic laugh came over me. I walked out the classroom door to relish in the moment and then, *whomp!*

I get hit in the face. Not by the cloaked spinster of darkness but by the foot of my buddy Todd. Just a moment before I stepped through time, Todd and Jimmy decided to have *an altercation* in the hallway. Jimmy had spun Todd and his size 14-and-a-halves around the hallway to meet my smiling right eye.

The part of my eye that later in life would hold bags from no sleep, now swelled nearly as high as a boy's pride for having such a wound. My eye had a lump under it like the rum keg under a Saint Bernard's chin. I could not hide it. I did not want to. The infamous Sister T finally returned and saw me immediately. I think she called me 'Mr. Morgan,' but I was probably caught up in the moment. "What happened to you?"

Everyone in the class knew exactly what happened, but I said, "I was coming up the stairs, sister, and someone opened the other double door'.

"Well, you need to go downstairs and see the nurse."

This is perfect. I got hurt. I did not rat on my friends. I had a badge of honor and everyone knew it. That is, except for one minor detail. Todd and Jimmy owned up while I went downstairs.

If I were Jewish, I would have called them "schmucks!" I think I will. Instead of a badge of honor I got to stay after school for lying with the schmuck brothers. It was my birthday and I would be late for my own party which was really only a home-made cake.

After I had stayed until the very end, I told Sister Thomas that it was my birthday to make her feel bad. She started to cry. She put her head down in her hands and wept for all the hateful things she had done to me. Okay, I was day-dreaming again. In reality, she handed me a cloth with ice for my eye which is the most sympathy anyone ever got from her since her old days in Salem, Massachusetts.

Naturally, with the biggest black eye ever, we had class pictures the very next day.

Okay, so I lied. I did not get away with anything, but I was a star for a moment.

The Morning Ride

You cannot have a two-mile ride, three bicycles, four boys and the freshly pressed vestments of an altar boy without a mishap, certainly not after a night's rain.

It was one of those beautiful Long Island spring mornings. I loved the smell of wet cement. The dodging of mud puddles made the ride to school at least enjoyable. Even the flowers seemed brighter, but that part is something I would not have shared out loud.

We'd meet at the standard and repeatable crossroads of our neighborhood. This was one schedule we kept. We would never be late, not for each other. Here we are. Four schoolboys clothed in light blue short-sleeved shirts over navy blue pants and knitted ties labeled SMS. We are biking our way to a school, a school a mere two miles away.

We are obviously a private-schooled and well-disciplined lot. Over each of our shoulders are the vestments of an altar boy, securely held by wire hangers, as the ends of the garments fly behind us like capes. Oh, how holy we are as we bicycle our way to their equally holy school of St. Mary's *Fairies*.

We opted not to take the bus, on this beautiful spring day.

On the handle bar sits, Billy, the younger brother of Todd who is not yet an altar boy. His feet are gently resting on the axle of the front wheel as he faces forward. Billy is a non-entity at this age, that is, until his foot slips into the front spokes.

The front wheel of the bike stops abruptly, pitching all of its contents forward, toppling books, vestments and all aboard, not to mention a plethora of pride. Todd used words like *plethora* because we were not allowed to say shitload.

But he did manage to yell, "You stupid son-of-a-bitch!"

"Isn't it ironic to call you little brother a son-of-a-bitch?" Dylan says only loud enough for me to hear.

"I guess bastard might have been worse," I replied with the same careful volume. After all, Todd was angry right now. No sense in pushing this button now. We would savor that fun for later.

How Todd's outfit miraculously missed the gigantic mud puddle was a mystery. No, his vestments opted for the greasy bicycle chain instead. With the normal sympathy of our age, we said, "Great! Now we're going to be late."

We gathered up the debris and set off for another happy day of being smacked around for being …" Tardy!"

Arriving Late

If the occasional bike malfunction did not make us late, we could always find another way. Even the most careful plans could not save us from the public ridicule from our beloved principal, Sister Disgusting.

Taking the bus to school got us there fifteen minutes early.

"It's bad enough they own us for seven hours. This is fifteen minutes of *our* time!" as we headed across the street.

Now that we were over twelve years of age we decided that a nice cup of coffee was required. To appreciate a morning lecture in an awakened state, caffeine was essential. So we would use this excess time to get what would later in life be known as *Starbucks*.

We had to drink it there because I don't think go-cups were invented yet. Besides, the last thing we needed was to bring back evidence of our side trip. We headed over to the school.

I am convinced that Bermuda has no monopoly on that triangle. For somewhere in the 300 feet between the coffee shop and the school, time warped. We left the luncheonette well on time, but still managed to arrive late, shaking our heads in disbelief. On such a day as this, Sister Agnes, a well-wrinkled principal and noted Dick Tracy character, did catch us.

Her lack of surprise was surely compensated by the distinct pleasure she took in having another opportunity to deliver punishment. She relished in this opportunity, which somehow, I felt, should have been a violation of some commandment. I swore to look that up later.

As was her practice, she gathered the entire school (do I exaggerate? No, I do not!), the entire school, to belittle us. And then she called the *Usual Suspects* by name to stand before her for the beating.

These lectures were often accompanied by some corporal slap or even an angry barrage of them. Usually, one slap per syllable of the lecture would do nicely sharing each of them among the four stooges.

"Oh, we happy few! We band of brothers!"[17]

"From the moment you step onto that bus, you belong to *ME!*" (Let's see, that was good for fifteen slaps).

One of us did make the mistake of blocking one of these slaps. Nobody in the history of St. Mary's had ever heard of a blocked slap much less seen one.

---

[17] From King Henry V, Saint Crispin's Day Speech by Wm. Shakespeare (who was probably not a Catholic or we would have learned about him.) I stuff like this in whenever I can to appear more educated.

Hey! One more day of detention was worth the incredible sound of the gigantic gasp uttered in harmony, by the entire school.

Yet in some strange way, your stature within the ranks moved up a couple of notches. Even the upperclassmen would say hi to you in the halls. You see, as is true with all handicaps, God compensates.

Blessed are the beaten for they shall also inherit detention.

8ᵗʰ Grade - Sister Zelda

Maybe it was justice or reward that gave us the oldest teacher to finish our last year at Saint Mary's. More likely Agnes felt that Sister Frances and her heart condition could not take us. You decide.

Sister Zelda was our 8th-grade teacher and was the first to teach science…strike that…the first to read science out of a book to us. Make that a strike two. She did not read it, we took turns reading it. She would underline the sentences that she was probably going to put on the test and tell us to do the same.

"Sister, I think I missed a few important paragraphs that I was supposed to underline."

She would lend us her book where she noted exactly what would be on the test. We'd pass that around. Some of the 'stupid' kids still failed.

Something Chocolate This Way Comes

She was pretty heavy and committed the mortal sin of eating chocolates behind an open book without sharing. We read out loud, but her mind was elsewhere, and usually, so were we. She was always on the wrong page. She could not turn a page with the box of chocolates there. We called her Zelda the Zombie. This made her the exception to the rule. We gave her a nickname, but we liked her. I guess we had no rules.

Reading Aloud

I am not sure where I overcame my shyness, but it certainly wasn't reading out loud at St. Mary's. This was a harrowing experience. I could read an entire paragraph perfectly while thinking of something else. I often did this so well I could not tell you what the paragraph was about at all. In a test, I would have to read the same thing over and over again to get my answer. My mind drifts so quickly. If I am not careful, it still happens today.

A number of our antics were built around our requirement to read out load as instructed. Sister Zelda would pick out a section in a history book and we would read one at a time, a paragraph or two and she would say "Next."

Up and down each row she went. Can you picture the perfect order of things as each student in their turn would read perfectly?

Petty and Maguire were speed readers before their day. They would count the number of paragraphs to figure which one was on your turn. Then they would catch a word or phrase to key on and wait for the right moment. You start to read aloud and they would interject a *whisper* only you could hear.

"The frontiersmen were walking through the woods when they were attacked by the Iroquois…

"Who were naked!"

"…uh….uh... Iroquois Indians. They walked quickly with their…

"Willies hanging out!"

Laughter blurts out of the reader, meaning me, "Sorry, Sister I ….I lost ….lost my place."

By the time you were done you were rung out and sweaty thankful that your time was over.

"So that's how it's going to be, eh. Well then let the *Games* begin. Revenge! Let's see five more paragraphs until Petty's turn. Then the sixth belongs to Dylan and they both belong to me!!!"

Petty was unflappable. Mere words and innuendo did not rattle him and, in fact, he might even spill your name out in the middle of his reading.

"The Iroquois were adept in their hunting…Wade…skills and made excellent use of the skins …" Petty went on.

He did have one weakness, one flaw, an opening if you will; he read with both hands under his table as he leaned forward. And so, I reached over to the 500-page text book and simply flipped the cover, closing all from his view. He rifled to find the page again as Sister Zelda finally looked up.

"Robert, please continue."

"Yes, sister!" and he plowed through the pages.

I whispered. *"It's only a couple of paragraphs after their willies were hanging out."*

And so it went in the perfect order of things as each student in their turn would read so perfectly.

JFK

My mother was very very active in politics. I did not realize how involved she was in the Democratic Party. She held no office. She was a committee woman and a hell of a fund raiser. I thought they meant fun-raiser. I *mistook* a lot of things in those days.

In 1960, JFK came to Long Island during his campaign. My mom took my friend Joe and I to see him. We were not even in the arena where he spoke. This sucks! We were standing on this flatbed truck in the sweltering heat of the summer, but we were ready with some confetti. We made it from ripped up newspapers. We saw something moving and Joe yelled, "He is coming toward us!"

Joe and I had sweated so much that the confetti Joe threw stayed in a ball. Instead of fluttering down like feathers, a sweaty paper ball bounced of JFK's head. He looked up. I let mine slip out of my hand onto the ground unnoticed hoping they won't dust for fingerprints.

He looked up and came right at us! He got up on the flatbed truck

"Uh… oh… sorry, mister!"

Kennedy smiled and looked at my mother instead and said, "Hello" and shook her hand like they were old friends, but they were not. He said hi to Mr. Raynor, too. He did not say hi to Joe or me because we hit him in the head with a big spit ball. I guess he figured that it would not be good to smack a 10-year-old off the side of the head in front of everyone, so he started to speak.

He talked like the people I saw in the summer in Vermont, I understood whatever he said, sort of. Somehow we felt closer to him. After all, I was already 10 and I had never met a celebrity before.

After I had heard my dad say that he would never beat Nixon, I knew he would be our next president. After all, my dad also rooted for the Red Sox. Unfortunately, he would never get to see them win a World Series.

JFK's picture hung on the wall at school. Did I mention that JFK was a Catholic? There might be a test on that later. We would hear about everything he did every day. It was all about vim and vigor. We had a President's Fitness Test we had to take. His wife was pretty and they were younger than the old people that were in the White House before them. They were like royalty, especially next to that ugly Russian guy.

My father was working a lot and making extra money, so we were set for another month in Vermont. This summer, we even got a newer car. Life was pretty good.

"This guy's not so bad after all," my dad finally admitted, 'It doesn't mean that I will vote for him though."

"Whew!" he had me scared there for a minute. I was hoping for another term.

We were sitting in class after lunch one sunny November day and Sister Zelda came back in the room looking rung out.

"The president has been shot," she said and she was shaking. We had television sets in the classrooms even back then. She closed the door and put the TV on. Walter Cronkite confirmed that in louder words.

It wasn't on long before the principal came and made us turn off the TV. It was the first time I felt sorry for the sisters, they were devastated. I wanted to hug them and tell them that everything was going to be okay. Well, not Agnes and Thomas but the other nuns.

I don't know if the buses came early, but we were headed home pretty quickly after that. No matter what they said on the television, we were sure that he would be okay. But it was not okay. He died that very day, November 22, 1963.

It wasn't so much that he was a Catholic, that he was young and good-looking, that he had that 'vim and vigor.' It was the very first time that we felt somehow connected to the president. An umbrella of safety had been shattered, an invincible hero had been taken away. The office of the presidency and the American people would never be quite the same. Somebody took this country down, someone with no respect for this country, someone who should burn in hell.

I guess we all know where we were that day. My face was buried at home in a pillow.

Less Than Proud Moments

These are among our less than proud moments. They cross the line of the sacrilegious, but they are confessions of insight into the deepest roots of our behavior

We said that there is an unspoken rule in humor that things are exponentially funnier in the most serious of places. The classroom was good, but there could be no more serious a place than a ceremony in church. At least there was one place where we drew the line, the altar. There would be no laughter unless the priest summoned it from the crowd in his sermon. Outside of the sanctity of the alta, there were no rules.

Our church could hold the entire school from kindergarten through the eighth grade. That's about nine-hundred or so *ready to snicker at the least little thing* kids in a serious place. This was a recipe conjured up by the devil himself. Add to that a dash of nuns, lay teachers and a priest who did not like snickering of any kind.

Ooh, did someone say *lay teacher?*

Our shoulders would convulse and our faces burst with redness as we tried to control another outburst. Suddenly from nowhere, there was a 'Smack' right in the back of the head. It was Thomas, the fastest wrist this side of the Pecos, "After School, the bunch of you!"

It's like the older kids would say, "Things could be a lot worse, you'll see."

The Stations

Those yellow flowers on the bushes were the first signal that the spring was here. I noticed lots of stuff like this that I would not admit to, not even to my partner, Alfred.

The weather was warming and I could smell the leather of baseball in the air. A few more hours of school and I'd be home to have a catch with the guys. First, we have to do the Stations.

I am not sure how often, maybe once a month or two, we would do the *Stations of the Cross*. This is a very respectful walk through all of the 14 Stations about the crucifixion of Christ. The solemn nine-hundred plus the eighteen mentioned above, would sit, stand and kneel as commanded by the priest. He led a procession of two candle-bearing acolytes and a more senior altar boy, who carried a large seven-foot cross.

I remember thinking that as holy as Sister Agnes and Sister, the Tommy-gun, Thomas believe they are, they will never get to do what I am doing. They will never get to assist in the mass or even go on the altar. I guess they feel they will get their revenge at the gates of heaven but not today.

On such a day as this, I had the honor to bear the cross, but only one more hour and I am outta' here.

A big center aisle runs from the front door all the way to the altar guarded by gray marble steps and a large brass rail. On the main floor, the students are in wooden pews and are split evenly, thirty rows on the right and thirty to the left, nearly every pew is packed. And so, the stage is set.

The church is beautiful with the angels painted up high in the clouds on a huge ceiling with a light blue sky. Off white marble columns are here and there to support the weight of the structure, a structure that would be put to a test. We proceeded to leave the altar down the center aisle following the priest. Each of the stations has a picture, a number, and a short title. The first station is only a few feet away from the steps, we stopped and turned right face.

The priest announces, "Jesus is Given His Cross."

He says a few more words, leads a few prayers and then, left face. Our small procession walks to the next station, and the priest says, "Jesus Falls for the First Time

Each time we right face, we look down the pew of solemn students where at the end up on the wall is the picture of each station. There are fourteen in all.

With every left face, we walked to the next station; with every right face, that cross remained steady as a rock.

Finally, I am almost home free. We are at the last station. I right face and look down the pew and there they are McBurke, Maguire, Backer, Petty and Post, you know, *The Boys*. There they are sitting exactly in line, not with the priest or the acolytes. Oh no, they have to be right there in line with me!!!

I must have looked so saintly, so pious and so serious. I was rapt in the moment and a task flawlessly delivered. It was too perfect and they could not bear it. Red-faced, shoulder-convulsing whispers that only I can hear. They were like a line of nearly exploding thermometers with their shoulders hunched and heads bobbing up and down like some hideous scene from Fantasia. I was standing there firm, defeating their every little quip.

"Look at them!" I thought. I almost had to laugh at their hideous attempts to make me falter. I almost had to laugh it was so hideous. And then it was so hideous! I could take it no more and slowly I began to lose it. Trying to regain my composure only to make things worse. The once steady cross now started to wave back and forth. If I had a white flag, it would have looked like I had surrendered, and surrender I did to the barrage of punches from both barrels of Sister Tommy-gun.

She was talking in tongues as each volley struck hard with only one discernible phrase, *"AND* if you think you are going to *Freedom Land*, you can forget it!!!"* I caught that because it was the most important thing she said.

So here it is. The one, the only good field trip of the year and I do not get to go. You see, if I were in public school, this would be no big deal. It would be only one of their trips.

The Wine and the Water

I am not sure if we had the discretionary taste to label the wine. It did have a label. I know it was not even a Mandave that was for sure. It did not taste like grapes, it tasted like dirt. We snuck it anyway simply because we weren't supposed to.

Isn't this true of most things. How awful was your first ciggy, or a sip of beer, or a shot of whatever? Your body wants to hurl it, but that wouldn't be cool.

So down it goes, and you'd say out loud, "Wow, that's great, isn't it!?!" but you're thinking, "I can always Ralph this up later when no one's looking."

For some unknown reason the next time it starts to taste 'not as bad' and the next time 'that's pretty good' and then you get older, and it becomes 'oh thanks, I needed that.' You see I have addiction down to a science now. I did notice one thing, this never happens with stuff like lima beans.

AA kept calling because I could not fill a crucible without taking a little sip. I always let Alfred fill the water. I am pretty sure I saw him sneak a sip of that. Hey, we didn't want anybody poisoning the priest, not on our watch!

We'd go through the checklist and make sure we had everything: the wine, the water and the bells. The bells were three gold ones in a golden triad. They were rung by at a certain point in the mass. Alfred liked ringing the bells and I would let him because I was a nice guy and a good partner. And he, being an equally good partner, would not say anything about my sip of wine.

Weddings and Funerals

As an altar boy, a usual tip for a wedding or a funeral back then was about $5. There were four of us at a funeral but only two at a wedding. Doing the math, a wedding was always better. Some times when the guy at the wedding felt generous, we would get $5 apiece. No one feels generous at a funeral.

Since my allowance was about a quarter, these events were like a gold mine. Yeah, weddings were definitely better. The brides were a lot better to look at than a box, well most of the time. That's a good thing too because a wedding is about as boring as a ceremony can get.

"Do you promise to make each other miserable... blah, blah, blah...?"

"They are really getting their five bucks worth," I thought.

We have to serve this mass and stand there through this boring exchange of vows, with people crying and noses blowing. It makes your feet hurt and your ears beg for mercy.

We would be facing the couple on either side of the priest. I liked the groom's side because then the bride and the bridesmaids were all looking in my direction. If I were on the other side, the priest would always have to give me a nudge to wake me up. I always winked at the bride even though she wasn't the one giving the tip.

After it was over, we would casually stand around outside with one palm up like we were expecting rain. "Wow, thanks, mister" or "Yeah thanks, thanks a lot" we'd say, depending on the tip.

Funerals were more impressive because there were four of us. We each had stuff to do and there is a lot more going on. In addition to the bells, there was an incense-filled thurible carried by an altar boy called the Thurifer. One of the priests would light it during the ceremony. I loved the smell of it and we would argue over who would get to hold it. With the right foursome, you could polish off half a bottle (of wine?) before the ceremony. And we would toast, "You can have the bells, Alfred."

Unlike weddings, funerals usually took place during school hours, so there was an added blessing. Sorry, an added benefit of getting out of class. I tried my level best not to look at the people crying because that could wrench your gut pretty hard. Alfred taught me that, "Don't look at them," he'd whisper. I tried to shrug it off like I was tough, but he was right. "Don't look at them."

We normally got our $5 to split up. Sometimes we would not get a dime. I guess it would be wrong to say, "Hey someone *stiffed* us!" but hey, 'wrong' never stopped me before.

171

Lesson 9: Other Antics

The tricks were purely and meticulously measured by what you could get away with. In Sister Thomas's case this was nearly zilch; in Sister Zelda's class, the world was Oysters Rockefeller.

Spit balls were for amateurs. Passing notes was for lovers, we wanted *action.*

Rubber Balls

As Sister Zelda would be writing on the blackboard, a pink Spalding rubber ball would bounce against the board, be caught and stowed away before she could turn around.

"Did anyone hear that?"

We all looked around as if we were about to tell a dirty joke.

"What, Sister?"

"Was someone knocking or hammering?" she'd ask.

"No, Sister."

A group of tell-tale circles left on the board like a murder of crows told the story. We would try to count them all for the record books, but then another ball would hit and we'd have to start over.

Spit Balls

I think this started in public school. There was something about it that did not feel very Catholic, parochial maybe, risky, most definitely.

Our private school version had an understandable twist to it. We did not shoot at each other, we had another target.

Because of the nun's habit, you could get a spitball to stay on her hood. This took an excellent shot for sure. The distance and the elevation had to be exact. But this was *so-worth-it*.

Just think! Watching her parade around with your spitballs on her shrouded head like a badge of honor, knowing that everyone in the class knew exactly where they came from, Ahhh.., we lived for such moments.

Unfortunately, I sucked at it. Not to mention the telltale pebbles of failure all over the floor. This required planning.

It took time to master, but where could one practice such a sport as this? I know. I could share with my friend Buddy. He'd figure a way. We'd practice. It was pretty disgusting, so we practiced it even more. A short straw is the weapon of choice because it is easier to hide, but the long straw puts a more accurate spin on the ball.

It was sure to become another Olympic sport someday. Well, maybe not a sport all by itself. I imagined myself skiing down a slope, stopping, shooting a few spit balls at Sister Zelda's hood and then continuing on down the hill to victory. I could see me on the podium with another gold medal for the good old US of A.

Practice told me that if I waited until she got to the board that I could bounce them off the wall over her head. You need a somewhat dry ball, one rolled in your hands with no spit or very little. It was not as disgusting, but some sacrifices must be made if you want perfection. This bounce off the wall deadened the speed and plopped it in place like a bird flying into a clean window.

One had to be careful though; too low on the wall and it could hit her in the face or in the eye. You wouldn't want that to happen. You might get caught.

I was getting too good for my britches. I should have stopped at five.

"Okay, who did that?"

Did I ever tell you that the person who says, "*What, Sister?*" is the first suspect.

Take a Powder

Until recent generations, the boards in the classrooms were made of black slate or slate-like materials. You wrote on them with white chalk, which was limestone-based. Later gypsum was introduced. Writing with that was smoother, but the dust was just the same.

We erased the chalk with a wooden block that had a felt cover. It was messy as hell and the white powder was uncontrollable.

It dried out your hands and got on the darks part of your clothes as if you freeloaded on the 3:10 to Yuma. If you erased the board, you made sure you wiped your hands, usually on someone else.

One of the disgusting punishments that we had was to go *clap the erasers*. This was something you did outside, downwind if you were born with some intelligence.

Eraser fights were frequent. They left well-defined marks. The nuns were chalk-splatter experts and could forensically define who did what to whom at what angle.

It was nasty stuff. It was so nasty that I would wash my hands *before* I went to the bathroom. This is a must if you want to be cool. It is hard for people to take your Bailey Strut seriously with a big white blotch around your fly.

The whole chalk thing brought forth a treasure chest of opportunity for pranks and antics. So at recess, we would find a planning spot in the schoolyard and figure our attack. Wiping away a smooth space of dirt we would make a makeshift diagram of the classroom.

Oh wait! I see. Now you doubt me. I can see the raised eyebrows. Fine. Okay, you got me. We did not plan, okay? We talked about what we would do and then we did it.

"I bet I can get two good eraser marks on the back of her habit today!" I said, "And she won't even notice."

Post makes little of my intended feat. "I can do three."

"Can't."

"Can!"

"I'll do four then," I said.

"I dare ya'."

Shoot, four was a lot.

"Okay, I'll do two after recess and two more before the end of the day."

"Okay, but we must be able to see all four, or it doesn't count."

What the hell did I get myself into? God, I am always doing this. I had a perfectly good plan ruined by my stupid prideful exaggeration. I was always moving the bar a little too high or pushing the line of death a little too close.

I got back to the classroom early and started cleaning the boards to make sure I had a fully loaded weapon.

"Well, thank you, Wade. What a pleasant surprise," Sister Zelda said as she took her seat and opened her book.

"You're welcome, Sister. I figured we would need the board for Science later," as I patted her lightly on the back.

Sister smiled at me boastfully as if she had finally made me a convert to her gentle fold. She was so happy that I almost felt guilty: two down, two to go.

A quick knock on the door woke me from my daydream. A knock and a quick open of the door could only mean one thing, our principal!

Sheer panic ran through me. I could feel the rush of terror building its pressure as it rose to my head, dragging my heart to my throat along with it.

"Please, please, oh please do not turn around, Sister!" I thought as I shot off a few Hail Mary's.

"I thought I'd stay for the science lesson to see how the class is doing," Sister Agnes said way too calmly.

You remember her; she's that really nice principal and devout nun that I was telling you about. Okay, okay, I am that desperate!! *Please dear God?*

Sister Zelda already standing, "Yes, Sister Agnes. Okay, class? We will open our books to Chapter 5, The Human Heart."

"Okay, now I am begging, do NOT draw any pictures on the board, please!" I begged quietly while doing a speed-rosary.

"Perhaps an illustration would be great here."

"Yes, Sister," as I jumped up, "I'll do it!"

For the first time in my life I finally knew what a brown-nosed, sissy-faggot must feel like. The utter disdain of the class felt like steel daggers in my back where my spine once held residence. None of them knew about the bet with Post. They had to wonder why I would take a reputation that took years to build and suddenly toss it aside like last year's Willie Mays. I took my book to the board and started to draw.

My first attempt at the left ventricle was nervously weak. I grabbed the eraser like a ripe opportunity. I moved it up and down on the board letting it slip through my fingers hitting Sister Zelda on the shoulder.

I picked it up from the floor and brushed off Sister Zelda's back.

"*SAVE!*"

I finished the drawing and got back to my seat.

Post leans over, 'You lose!"

"So what," I said as I am thinking about the 2 rosaries I promised.

Then Sister Agnes picked up the floor board and drove the final stake through the telltale heart of my reputation, "Very nicely done, Wade," she said as she left the room.

I might as well buy a hat with some nice earmuffs and skip around at recess yelling, "Hey! I'm a fully licensed sissy. Someone kick the crap out of me, please!?"

Put Your Name on the Board

Sister Zelda could not possibly keep track of all of our ill-doings during the day. And so, she devised a method, a plan 'that will live in infamy.'

For your first offense, she would tell you to go to the back of the room and put your name on the board. We had a long blackboard on her left side of the room that ran all the way to the back. It is there at the very back, that you would put your name for all prosperity, or at least until the end of the day. If you happened to commit another offense, you had to put a check mark next to your name.

Todd leaned over and smacked me in the back of my head while I was reading out loud, but he got caught.

"McBurke!! Put your name on the board."

"Yes, Sister."

And to the back of the room Todd would go, he found his name was already there, so he wrote 'ROBBINS" instead. Todd's face turned the habitual tell-tale red, so we checked out what he had done and performed the ritual snickering. Poor Steven, he did not do anything. Well, at least he'd get the honor of staying after with the *Boys*.

"Maguire!" Sister Zelda said as she watched his every move. "Put your name on the board!"

Dylan stood up. "Yessss, Sisssster Zell-dahr," as he pronounced every elongated syllable.

Sister Zelda put her nose back in her book and snuck a few more hidden chocolates in her mouth.

It seemed that several minutes passed by before Dylan drew enough attention to finally move. But instead of heading to the back of the room where the blackboard was, he went towards the front. He took the long way up and down each row milking the Bailey Strut for all that it was worth.

When he finally reached the board, he grabbed the chalk and swiped the air like Art Carney before signing a contract.

And then he leaned over from the waist and wrote his name in the tiniest of indiscernible letters as Sister Zelda finished her last bonbon.

"BIGGER! SO I can see THEM!" she yelled.

"Yes, Sister."

He erased his tiny effort and proceeded to take up the entire set of blackboards with each new stroke. When he was done only one giant letter, M existed with no room for another.

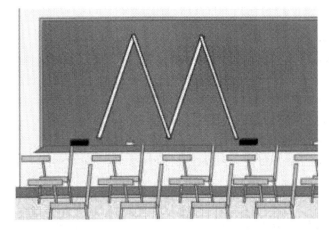

'NORMAL-sized and JUST FOR THAT put 2 check marks next to it!"

"Yes, Sister."

He erased it all and put two check marks next to Robbins name and strutted back in the same path as before.

"Wade!" Sister Zelda said as she caught me passing a note to Christine. "Let me see that."

Backer passed me a blank piece of paper as I walked passed him and I handed it to Sister Zelda. *I pocketed the real one.*

"What's this?" she asked.

"I didn't have time to write anything, Sister."

She closed one eye entirely and cocked her head, "Go put your name on the board."

I didn't press my luck. I wrote my real name and then put 2 check marks next to Robbins.

We always had detention, but we called it 'staying after.' After a while, the bus driver did not wait or even ask about us anymore. We stayed even when our names were not on the board out of habit.

I never understood the check marks because you had to stay after school no matter how many you had. I think you just stayed longer. One time I had so many check marks I slept there for a year and shared a cell with Robbins.

I dreamed that one day we would be so famous that they would rip that board off the wall and it would be hung in a museum, like one of those war monuments.

How Do I Get into Trouble

Let me count the ways. When you think about it, the Ten Commandments are a beautiful piece of work. In ten small sentences they encompass *every* possible sin. *Every* possible wrong can be traced back to one of these platitudes...sorry, I meant teachings. If you follow every single one of these, you will never get into any trouble whatsoever.

Yeah, right.

Within the very mind of every child is a cookie waiting to be taken, a cookie, not calling, but shouting to be taken. A cookie that tastes so good because of the unsolicited freedom that you have bestowed upon it. All I need is a ladder and that cookie is mine. All I need is a loophole and the keys to the city are mine.

I think that this is the exact reason why man invented congress. But we do not have to pay four hundred men without principles to find loopholes, hell, a nine-year old can do that.

Oh, yes they can!

I think you have learned enough so far, so tell me, which commandment says, *"Thou shall not snicker"* or *"Thou shall not make people snicker"*?

Nope, not there! Snickering is therefore allowed. Otherwise there would be another commandment for it. However, I do think, "Thou shalt not covet thy neighbor's snicker" is covered.

It is the one about 'thy neighbor's goodies.' You are not allowed to covet those. You can touch their goodies and get smacked, but you can't covet them.

"Thou shalt not laugh at stupid people." Nope, not there. These are all free reign and so much more.

What if I take Peter's hat, antagonize him until he cries and give it back to him?

"Thou shalt not borrow." Nope, not there either, so all is good.

So now, let me ask you, is taking money that does not belong to you a sin? Well, let's see. There is a commandment that says,

"Thou shalt not steal."

But, if someone *gives* you the money, I mean just hands it over to you, it is not stealing. I mean, if a kid hands over some baseball cards to be my friend, it is not stealing. It is a friendly gesture. It is what Congress calls, lobbying for your friendship. So we are not breaking any commandments here. We are staying within the *guidelines* laid out by those who set their excellent example.

This is the divine right of private schooling. These years of practice and education assure you a seat in politics, or its close relation, prison. It is critical that you see how this works. It is equally important that you agree with me so I can retain my delusion that someday I will go to heaven.

"Thou shalt not piss off a penguin." Nope, not there either.

It must be great to be a nun. You know exactly what you can and cannot do. You don't have to think when you are on the playground like we did. You stand there with your arms folded wondering, 'why me?"

We, on the other hand, had to follow our rules on the fly. Most of what we did was not covered, so you had to think fast. I don't want to burn in hell. So, I would think, is what I am about to do okay? Is it a sin? I'd carefully scan those ten special sentences, find one that applies, pick apart every word and then rationalize your righteousness.

"Nope, not covered. This is okay," as I'd push Alfred down the hill.

You see what a gray area this is? You need to dig deep into your dark side to weigh all this out. This is why God made lawyers. I often wondered why more lawyers aren't Catholic. Later in life, I figured it out.

You become a lawyer because your mother made you feel guilty for not becoming a doctor like your brother did. That's really a Jewish thing. The Christians had nothing left to do, but fill their void in politics. If you are a terrible liar, you become a Democrat. If you are a great liar, you become a Republican. That's just the way it is, and so it is written.

Lesson 10: Another World Outside

Recess

Public schools had a gymnasium, we had a yard. Now that I reflect on it, this was to prepare us for our later life in prison.

The population was let out at the ring of a bell around 12:00 Noon. We did not have a cafeteria either. We were not sure what this prepared us for so we brought our lunch. We'd rifle down a peanut butter and jelly, drank the milk the school gave us and started playing with something or somebody.

The winter was the best. In clear violation of the first commandment, we worshipped the snow plow gods. The school and the church shared this gigantic parking lot and they would pile it up making one huge mountain of snow. We were only allowed to play on the far side of this hill because the nuns told us, "don't let us see any of you on that hill!"

Ever play king-of-the-hill with 100 kids? I don't care if you broke something. If you got hurt, you had to suck it up. I bet public school didn't have big snow hills in their fancy gymnasiums. They did build a gym after we graduated probably in our honor, or at the very least, because of us.

Speaking of games we had certain rules we should call 'How to be a School Yard Victim.' You would surely be beaten up if you did any of the following:

1. You call yourself James, not Jim or Jimmy.
2. If you wore a hat other than a baseball cap.
3. Earmuffs, need I say more.
4. You run or walk like a girl.
5. You tattle on someone.

Girls were exempt from the rules, but even they had their own punishments for number five.

When we didn't have the hill, we had to invent games. Like antagonize-a-sissy, steal-Jonathan's-hat, can-you-take-a-punch or say something to Christine until she kicks your shins. This was certainly no substitute for the snow mountain. The spring really sucked.

If you got caught doing something wrong they made you pick up all the litter after recess. Are you kidding me!!? We would be *outside* picking up papers while the rest of the kids went back into the classroom *inside*?! This was the start of the new, end of recess game, called *Smack Each Other in Front of a Nun.*

"You will stay out here until all of those papers are picked up and don't forget about the side yard!"

Clearly, they did not think this punishment out fully? We milked it.

Field Trips

Every year the nuns would take us on a contained visit to the outside world. They would call it a field trip. We would also have a movie that we would see with them in the annex we called 'The Hall.'

The Hall was in the shape of a garage but much bigger. I'd say it was about 90 feet long and 30 feet wide. It could not hold the entire school, but even a half was crowded. The stage was about 3 feet off the ground so at least you could see the heads of the people in the film. We sat for hours in wooden folding chairs that were strictly forbidden by the Geneva Convention.

The movie was usually *King of Kings* or *The Robe,* you know, something religious. One particular year, however, we walked to a real movie theatre down the block. It was the East Littleton Movie Theatre with cushy chairs and the smell of popcorn, which we were not allowed to have. There was a big screen you could see from top to bottom. If that was not enough of a treat, the movie we saw was not religious.

Our Sister told us, "You are going to see *Seven Brides for Seven Brothers.*" I like the way that they put things. "You are going to see…" As if they were going to see something else.

"How cool!!" we thought.

"It is a musical."

"Okay, not cool," we rethought.

Indeed it was a musical from the get-go. It was romantic and all the guys pretended they would hate it. We could not have any candy either. So we had nothing to throw at each other when the lights went out. Any chance that a nun would know which one of us said or threw *what or from where*, dimmed along with the lights. We were ready for a little mayhem, but then the movie started and everyone went "*shhhhhhh!*"

It was kind of a western. This guy was singing about beautiful hides. He met this pretty woman who sang too, so they had to get married.

His six brothers were called backwoodsmen because they never bathed until the singing guy's wife made them. After that, she made them a nice breakfast. They liked the breakfast so much that they went out to steal some women of their own. This is where it got good.

We were mesmerized by six more beautiful girls and the cool backwoods guys that stole them. There was a scene where the girls ran around upstairs in their underwear they called *petty coats*. They didn't look too shabby to me. I know the nuns were embarrassed and had no idea of this scene beforehand. We did more than just snicker and, in the cover of darkness, we got away with it, a very notable event.

Anyway, the backwoodsmen and their girls started singing, but then they stopped when this baby showed up. Then everybody stopped singing and they all had to get married. It was the last outside movie we ever got to see.

It did not matter. We loved that movie and I watch it now and again with a grin and a snicker. I know, I know. It's a bad habit.

Ice Capades

Our yearly trips usually took us in or close to New York City. We called it the 'city' and everyone knew what we meant. It seemed we had to take a train to anywhere that was fun.

The trains had huge diesel locomotives that smelled like our bus from the back. It had a whistle you could hear a mile away and those old Pullman cars. The cars were different shades of gray on the outside, except for the caboose which was red. The inside was all tan and brown and it smelled like cigarette smoke and old sweaty commuters. It was dirty. We did not care. We were out of school and could barely contain ourselves for the hour ride.

Sometimes it would be the Ice Capades, but our favorite place was Freedom Land. It is not that we did not like some of the ice skaters. We liked them a lot.

The girl skaters did not wear very much. We were ten-year-old boys. We knew more at that age than our parents would dare to admit. We tried to sneak downstairs to their dressing room because Dylan said that it would be worth getting caught. Okay, we were hoping to see naked girls, but a little nudge from Old Dylan was good enough for me. We did get to see the door open and close and "there were flashes of pink and undefined nudity, but nothing I could *put my finger on*" as Todd said. Todd was our poet laureate.

Mark this one down. We did not get caught. The rest of the 'Capades' could not beat that.

Freedom Land

Freedom Land was much more than a park. It was loaded with great rides, cotton candy, soda and the most important thing of all, free time on our own. In retrospect, it was a parking lot with small buildings for food, haunted houses and a bunch of very cool rides. It was so dirty that if my little brother dropped his candy, even he would leave it.

We did not have beautifully green, landscaped, pansy, la-ti-da, sissy parks. We had dangerous rides that could break at any time. They had no seat belts and if you fell out, you could not sue anyone. I am talking *real* rides.

This was like Christmas. I could not sleep the night before and my legs ached in anticipation.

"I suppose you would rather see Freedom Land than the Bishop?" Sister Thomas said out loud.

(Aside) "This is a trick question. Don't answer it."

We met at the Littleton train station to get to Freedom Land. Here comes that smelly beast with the big caboose (referring to the train) that is going to take us to Freedom Land.

I could see Sister Disgusting staring in our direction. No doubt she is telling the other nuns what trouble they can expect from us. It is a wonder why they never gave a thought to separating the 'Three M Company.' They could not seem to break the alphabetic order of things.

As we took our seats, our close friends accepted the seats we had reserved for them.

"Can I sit here?"

"No."

This polite exchange would repeat itself until all were assembled then we'd throw things at each other for an hour. We were actually pretty good. After all, it was in our best interest.

The train slowed for the last time. A gigantic sign waved across the sky saying the words we came to revere, 'Freedom Land.' The irony of the term may have escaped us, but our actions were louder. It must have been June because it was already blazing hot outside as we stepped off the train.

Father Henry led us toward the gate. I guess he was chosen because he was from Brooklyn. The nuns followed us like shepherds.

"Let's all meet back here at *blah, blah, blah*," said Father Henry.

We all figured that one of us heard what he said and we were off.

Our pockets were bulging with paper route money; a sure ticket for trouble on an empty stomach. We each got two hot dogs and a coke while we planned our attack on the park. Someone got a map and we threw that in the garbage right away.

"What are you kidding me? Men don't need maps." After all, we were blessed with ball-bearings.

We walked until we found a ride we liked and got on line. Maybe some of the rides would be lame by today's standards. There were rusty fences and a rusty man at the gate to go with each rusty ride. There was no fancy Chinese red lead paint all over them. It was lead paint all right, but it was American lead paint. We did not have any reason to chew on it, so it was no big deal back then.

Their roller coaster was called the Might-Mouse which was a ninny name without the 'Y.' It went about a thousand miles an hour and made a left turn, upside down, three times. You had to watch your money because this ride would shake it out of you.

We had go-carts you rode solo, and remember, no seat belts. You had to be responsible for your own safety and the rides were better for it. Imagine, riding your own car at 11 years old? There was a height requirement and try as I might I could not make it. The guys all went without me and I went back for another run at the Might-Mouse.

I felt weird being alone. I mean there were only a few cars and they were full of kids. Some were from my school and they had to wonder why I was alone. We took off with a thud and the sound of the chain carrying us up the slope. Once again, I could see the entire park and the go-carts the guys were probably in. God, I hated being short. "Damned polio," I said out loud and then whoosh, down the slope toward the first corner.

Slamming into the turn like it hit something, the car rocked violently until it regained its wheels. We had been upside down for a second before that turn. It really feels like a different ride this time. Heading into the next turn, I waited for the slam, but the car did not turn. Instead, I lurched forward holding onto the bars. The car went up on its end and came down and then finally we all got our *Slam*.

Some of the cars are off the tracks. Everyone is okay. Those cars were built to take a beating. So the ride is broken and luckily I did not shit my pants. You never want to miss out on a chance to scare the crap out of the little kids that are with you.

"I hope there isn't another bunch of cars behind us!" I said.

We were right over the entrance after that turn, so it did not take long to get us down. You think they would have at least given us a free ticket or a soda. They were more concerned about our physical condition then to think of the essentials.

The go-carts are a popular ride. I guess the guys had to wait in line a while, but they were out there now. By the time they got in my story had started to grow out of proportion as I told them how I was thrown from the coaster about a hundred feet and there was blood all over. For all my effort all I got was a, "Yeah, yeah sure."

"Well you should a' been there," I said.

Their sympathy was replaced by great stories about the go-cart ride, which they were allowed to exaggerate together, to make me feel even better.

"Hey, you know," as I looked around "F_ _ k you guys." Some people look both ways before they cross the street, we did it before we cursed.

"Well, you shoulda' been there," they laughed.

I was more shaken than I admitted and was leery about the rest of the rides after that.

"Let's get something to eat."

"Good idea."

The cotton candy was five cents and it was bigger than two of our heads put together. You had to be careful especially near the rides. The wind will take that cotton and send to parts of your body that you don't want to be sticky. Hair is the worst.

More soda, more hot dogs, ice cream, candy and a few more rides were needed, before the train ride home.

"Hey let's try the Crazy House," I said, and we all went in.

It was peculiar. Everything looked and felt tilted. How did they do this? I could not walk across the floor without falling. This was too way close to polio for me.

(*Aside*) "Oh crap! I am turning into a wimp."

"Hey, guys. Let's go on a ride." I said.

My fears drifted away with each ride, but I would not go near a roller coaster for most of my life.

One of us actually did hear Father Henry, or we asked someone. Whatever it was, we got back to the gate just in time. It was a great day and we talked about it all the way home. A couple of kids wanted to know about the roller coaster accident.

"It was no big deal," I said as the guys all looked at me. "No one got hurt." This made everyone lose interest pretty fast.

I remember that year with a great smile, but the year that I did not get to go, that year still sticks in my craw.

The Year I Did Not Go

Todd and I had paper routes whose streets backed up to each other. The day I did not get to go to Freedom Land because I was punished, I did both routes. You will have to refer to the *Stations of the Cross* story to see why.

There were almost 100 papers, but I had to finish them all in a hurry. This way I would have time to meet Todd and Dylan when the train pulled into the station.

These paper routes were more profitable than the one I had in town. The only real place to waste your money was at the local Carvel on Todd's route. Wielding a bike full of papers while licking the drips off an ice cream cone takes practice and my bike had the scars to prove it.

Todd had a very unique batch of customers on his route. There were these two girls who yelled "hi' behind closed doors and giggled. We never saw them. There were less than the mandatory number of nasty dogs on his route, but there was this vicious rooster that made up for it. Let us not forget the lady who would come to the door less than half-dressed on collection days. Unfortunately, this was not a Friday. I knocked anyway to let her know the paper was there if she wanted it. My second favorite was Mrs. Leave-a-fart. Todd pronounced her real name to correct me, an annoying habit of his, by the way.

We would knock on her door, "Collect."

She had to be about ninety-years-old and she would always come to the door and say the same thing in rehearsed English and a feeble voice.

"I have no *money*... (hesitation)...I cannot *pay* you..."

This would be followed by a modest bow of her silver head and a flatulent sound. We hoped the sound was from the door closing. She owed Todd for three years of delivery. Her son finally paid Todd one day with a handsome tip. I think Todd retired after that. Anyway, it's time to go meet the guys at the train station.

Piles of excited kids got off. I looked at every one of them, but where were they? Did I miss them? I asked a few kids, but they were too young to know anything. Then I saw a nun. She turned. It was our beloved principal. She looked like a sun-dried white grape that someone sucked the pit out of and stuck back in a habit.

"Good Afternoon, Sister," I said to Sister Agnes so respectfully. "I did not see Todd or Dylan, Sister."

"Your friends!?! Your friends did not see fit to make it to the train on time!!! They will be on the next train with Father Henry and they can expect ample punishment tomorrow."

She's not fooling me. I know what was really pissing her off. She was ticked way beyond compare because I was not with them. I was not with them so she could not punish me for this one.

"If you were not already punished you'd be with them!" she added.

You see. I told you so. She was absolutely right. So I lashed right back at her.

"Yes. Thank you, Sister."

I rode off feeling like I had gotten away with something.

The Next Morning

Since I did not want to repeat the conversation with Father Henry, I did not come back to meet that next train. I caught up with the boys in the morning. They told me of the glorious adventures that I had missed.

When they realized that they had missed the train and would be punished anyway, they went on a thousand more rides. They ate more candy and each had 20 more hot dogs until Father Henry found them.

"You should have been there. And you're tall enough to ride the go-carts now! You should have seen them. They were even better than last year."

I must have been beet red.

"Okay, you say that again and someone is going to die today!"

When we got to school all of the boys (minus one) had to go to the principal's office. This sounds ridiculous, but between the swashbuckling tales of the missed adventure and now being left out of this? It was more than I could bear.

Somewhere within the six hours that followed I would manage to get in trouble again. Maybe it was intentional.

I certainly found a way to get punished and stay after with the guys. But what about tomorrow? They have to stay the whole week!? I'll think of something.

After all, I did not want to hear about a stop at Sleepy Hollow Lake and Kevin's latest mishap secondhand with another, "Hey, you shoulda' been there!"

Graduation

There are some things that you think that you would never admit. It was true that as the school year ended that I could hardly wait. That's easy. But, each year as September approached I could not wait for school to start again. This I would never admit.

Maybe it was because I was going into the next grade and welcomed the increased stature that came with it. Maybe it was seeing old friends. The truth is that I liked school, but it is like one of those stupid bowling leagues. It is fun in the beginning, but in nine months you're sick of it.

As graduation approached, it was with mixed emotions. There was something very 'last chance' about the days that remained. We were now the oldest in the school. Everyone knew who we were. We had respect, but it was almost over. We did not look ahead that far, but next year no one would even notice us. We would have to start all over again building a reputation in an unfamiliar world.

We had to practice standing in line by height. Sounds easy enough except for the fighting over whom was taller. We also had to practice walking up the aisle in church, to genuflect, as we had done so many times before, and to take our seats.

There were no antics this time. We were deep in our own thoughts about an end of an era. For once, we did as we were told and when the final day came the nuns cried. I guess extreme joy will do that to you.

We reexamined our scars where open wounds once lay. This was our closure. It was like the first time you jumped into deep water, not sure of your capabilities but profoundly stupid.

Wake up! Just take the good fortune of going on to public school where life is beautiful all the time and shut up about it. As for St. Mary's...

"Goodbye Old Friend"

History of St. Mary's

Most of the places, names and depictions have been renamed to protect the rights and feelings of the innocent and the not-so-innocent. This history, however, is typical of the times and applies to the growth of many small parishes during what was called a simpler time.

St. Mary's, East Littleton[18] was founded in the late 1890's, but the history of St. Mary's goes back to more than 50 years earlier

During the early 1800's, the Catholics in the Littleton area attended Mass, whenever possible, at St. Patrick's in Huntsville many miles away. Transportation was minimal and attendance was difficult and at times impossible from Littleton.

On July 29, 1853, Pope Pius IX established the Diocese of Brooklyn under the leadership of Bishop John Loughlin. It was Bishop Loughlin who enabled a missionary priest to celebrate Mass in the Outlying areas such as Bay City and the Littleton area

---

Around 1880, a group of Littleton and East Littleton Catholics purchased the old St. Luke's Episcopal Church for about $500 and moved it to the site of the present St. Mary's.

Three years later a pastor of was named for St. Anne's in Bay City and St. Mary's became a mission of St. Anne's. Now attendance by Littleton was easily achieved within a few miles

In the summer of 1898, St. Mary's was established as a parish. The first congregation numbered only 150 people.

In 1901, ground was broken for the present church. It was completed in the summer of 1902 at the cost of $15,000. The church seated 500 people.

In 1905, the first pastor was transferred to Brooklyn. It was this second pastor that built the first St. Mary's school. The original teachers of the school were lay persons. It was not until 1914 that the School Sisters of Our Lady arrived. The school opened in September of that year with 160 students.

St. Mary's saw a number of new pastors over the next 40 years. Each served their full time as each one passed. By 1950 there were 400 students in St. Mary's school.

(Our Story starts here, a brief segment in the school's history.)

In 1954, the pastor was moved to Westerly and Fr. Joseph Shatner became pastor. In 1955, the choir was formed under the direction of Edward Mallory. In 1957, ground was broken for a new school.

(We moved into that new school in third grade which would have been September 1958)

Fr. Shatner died in 1961 and was followed by Fr. James McCredie. By the time of his arrival, there were more than 2,700 Catholic families in the parish. There were almost 1,000 students in the school, 1,000 children in Religious Education programs, and 15 Sunday Masses. It was Fr. McCredie who began plans for the expansion of the school.

(This must refer to the 2nd expansion into the parking lot after the 1957 school was already built. The building was not erected until 1965 as stated below.)

Fr. McCredie left St. Mary's in 1963. Fr. William O'Sullivan came to our parish that same year.

(Our story end's in 1964 upon graduation.)

Bibliography

Bells of St. Mary's	"The Bells of St. Mary's" (1945) Rainbow Productions - American film tells the story of a priest and a nun who set out, despite their good-natured rivalry, to save a school. Starring Ingrid Bergman and Bing Crosby.
Boomer	Norman Julius "Boomer" Esiason (born April 17, 1961) is a former American football quarterback and current network color commentator.
Carol O'Connor	John Carroll O'Connor (August 2, 1924 – June 21, 2001) best known as Carroll O 'Connor, was an American actor. This Carol O'Connor reference is to a character he portrayed known as Archie Bunker; a veteran of World War II, reactionary,

bigoted, conservative, blue-collar worker, in a TV show called All in the Family (1971-83).

Darwin Award
A Darwin Award is a tongue-in-cheek honor named after evolutionary theorist Charles Darwin. Awards have been given for people who "do a service to Humanity by removing themselves from the gene pool" (i.e. lose the ability to reproduce either by death or sterilization in a stupid fashion).

Green Arrow
Green Arrow is a fictional super-hero, published by DC Comics in 1941 by Mort Weisinger and George Papp. He is an archer, who invents trick arrows with various special functions.

Ice Capades
The Ice Capades, founded in 1940 in Pennsylvania, was a traveling show often appearing in Madison Square Garden in New York City. They featured woman skaters in theatrical performances on ice.

Jonas Salk	Jonas Salk (October 28, 1914 – June 23, 1995) was an American medical researcher and virologist, best known for his discovery and development of the first safe and effective polio vaccine.
Leave it to Beaver	"Leave It to Beaver" was a 1950s and 1960s family-oriented American television situation comedy about an inquisitive but often naïve boy named Theodore "Beaver" Cleaver (portrayed by Jerry Mathers).
LoJack	LoJack: A System used in conjunction with law enforcement agencies for the recovery of stolen vehicles.
Matt Dillon	Matt Dillon. Nee Matthew, Actor, February 18, 1964. Originally a teen actor, Matt usually played troubled youth rolls.
Mickey Mantle	Mickey Charles Mantle (October 20, 1931 – August 13, 1995) was an American baseball center fielder and Hall of

Famer who played 18 seasons in Major League Baseball for the New York Yankees.

Palmer Method   The Palmer Method of penmanship instruction was developed and promoted by Austin Palmer in the early 1900s. It soon became the most popular handwriting system in the United States.

Phil Mickelson   Philip Alfred Mickelson (born June 16, 1970) is an American professional golfer. He is nicknamed "Lefty" for his left-handed swing, even though he is otherwise right-handed.

Pretty Woman   Pretty Woman is a 1990 romantic comedy film. Written by J.F. Lawton and directed by Garry Marshall, the film stars Richard Gere, Julia Roberts, and Hector Elizondo.

Richard Gere   American film star, born in Philadelphia on August 31, 1949, is a descendant of the Mayflower Pilgrims. He was actually born of Methodist parents.

Robert Frost	An American poet (March 26, 1874 – January 29, 1963). Considered to be the greatest American poet and author of poems such as 'Road Not Taken.'
Twilight Zone	Twilight Zone was a popular TV Series (1959-64) created by Rod Serling. They were a mixture of 30-minute self-contained fantasy, science fiction and suspense stories.
Wikipedia	Wikipedia: Thanks to Wikipedia for a wealth of Information on people, items and dates from their site at www.wikipedia.com.
William Shakespeare	William Shakespeare (baptized 26 April 1564; died 23 April 1616) was an English poet and playwright. The reference here is to the famous motivational St. Crispin's Day by King Henry V in the play by the same name.

Willie Mays

Willie Howard Mays, Jr. (born May 6, 1931) is a retired Hall of Fame American professional baseball player who played the majority of his major league career with the Giants.

About the Author

You remember the guy who was captain of the team, the president of the class, voted best looking and got all the girls. Wayne explains, "Yeah, I was his best friend."

To overcome his shyness he would pull pranks, tell jokes and even joined the drama club, but mostly he was and still is driven.

Christina LaFortune of Florida Today has featured this author. "Wayne J. Martin of Melbourne Beach, writes for the reader's amusement. He uses his sense of humor to showcase life's odd characters and their misadventures."

Originally from Islip, Long Island, Wayne now resides on a barrier island off the east coast of Florida. He says, "I'm drawn to islands and small towns. People smile a lot here; some say it's the salt in the air. I'd say it's because every day is Saturday."

You may order his books online, or you may order them through your local book store. Visit him at Amazon books author's page.

https://www.amazon.com/Wayne-J-Martin/e/B0092P73E0

Other Books by Wayne

"The Wobble" (series)

Novel: Science Fiction/Baseball

Book 1: Baseball and nature meet science fiction head-on in this story of power, greed, murder and revenge. In the face of Armageddon and threat of the earth's final days two young ball players stumble on an undiscovered law of physics.

"Knowing Jack"

Humor/Memoirs/Biography
Previously released as 'How to Give Up Golf'

Humorous stories about characters and their behavior on the golf course which for some may be too close to home. If you are buying it as a gift, you might wish to get a highlighter ready. If you receive this as a gift, please pay attention to the highlighted sections. If you are reading this for the humor, well then, that is even better.

Reviews

5.0 out of 5 stars - Ahhhh to be young again!
By **author** MJ Butler on October 4, 2012
Format: Kindle Edition | Verified Purchase

This book is chalk full of great memories of growing up in small town America. I loved it! Whether one went to parochial school or not, the antics of these youngsters will cross-relate. The characters in this book are endearing, and I found myself laughing out loud and also being transported back in time. I would liken the memoir-style recollection of this author's younger days to the style of the late, great Jean Shepherd. I enjoyed every page and every daydream as told through the eyes of this very talented writer who lived it himself. What a fun story and much appreciated walk down memory lane!

5.0 out of 5 stars - Still Snickering
By Shari on March 6, 2017
Format: Kindle Edition | Verified Purchase

This is a very funny account of growing up in the 50's and 60's, going to Catholic school and being an Altar Boy. It is a young boy's account of having nuns for teachers. … I read in bed at night and at one point my wife said, "What in the world is shaking the bed?" I had to confess it was me, in fact I'm still snickering.

Made in the USA
Columbia, SC
23 November 2019